The
Cathedral
of Seville

The Cathedral of Seville

Luis Martínez Montiel
Alfredo J. Morales

Scala Publishers
in association with
Aldeasa S.A.

The Cathedral of Seville
Text © Copyright Alfredo J. Morales 1999
Photography © Fotografías Arenas, 1999 and
© Santiago Moreno, 1999, pages 10, 21, 33 (right), 40-41, 76, 84, 93, 108

First published in 1999
by Scala Publishers Ltd
143-149 Great Portland Street
London WIN 5FB

ISBN 1 85759 203 4

Edited and designed by Grapevine Publishing Services, London
Translated from the Spanish by Isabel Varea
Printed and bound in Spain by Fournier A. Graficas S.A.

Photographic credits: All the photographs used in this book were supplied
by Fotografías Arenas, except for those on the pages above, that are credited
to Santiago Moreno.

Contents

THE CATHEDRAL OF SEVILLE
GENERAL PLAN

Based on an original plan by A. Fernandez Casanova (1890)

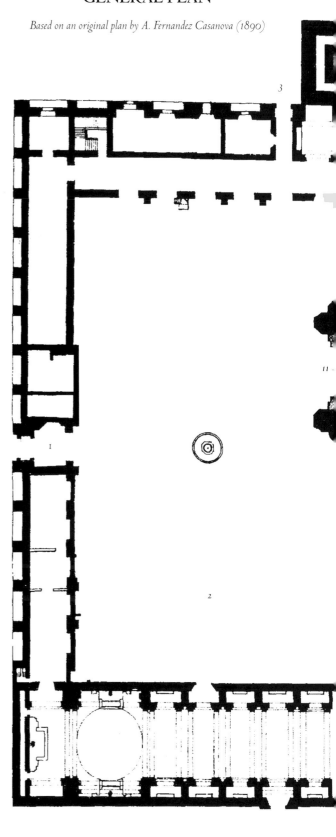

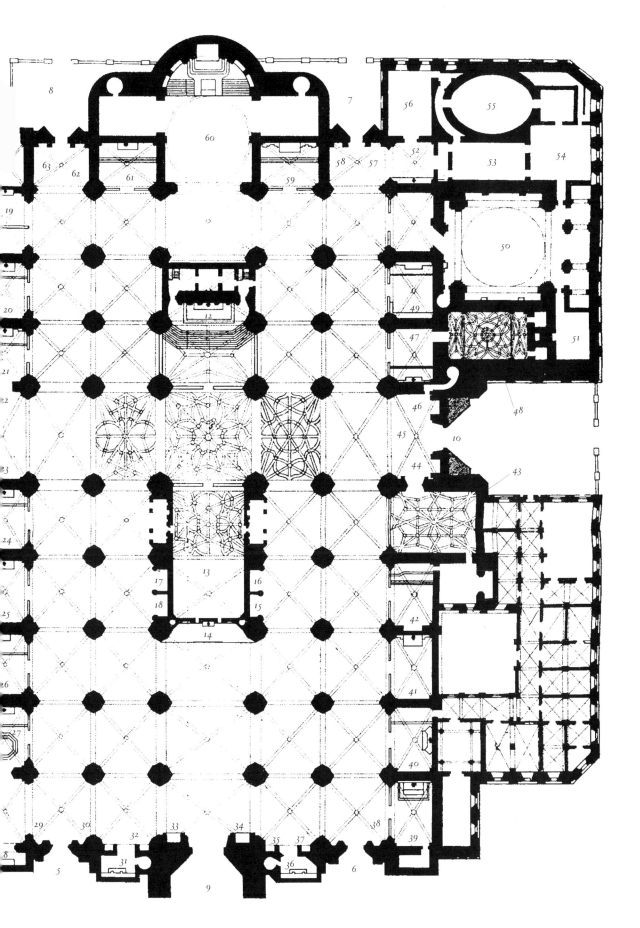

From Almohad Mosque to Christian Cathedral

After Seville had become the capital of the Almohad empire, the caliph, Abu Yaqub Yusuf, embarked on a major building programme in the city. One of the most significant projects was the construction of a much larger mosque. Building began in 1172, under the supervision of the architect Ahmad ben Basso, but came to a standstill four years later. When work was resumed in 1184, it was decided to build a minaret (now known as La Giralda) at the north-east corner of the prayer hall. The prayer hall consisted of seventeen aisles running from north to south, with the central aisle wider and higher than the rest. The outermost aisles on either side were extended to close off the eastern and western sides of the courtyard, where the faithful performed their ritual ablutions before entering the mosque. The north side of the courtyard was closed off by a single gallery. The mosque was built of brick with plasterwork decoration, and was supported by pillars with ironwork horseshoe arches. The roof above the aisles was made of wood. A series of doors led to both the ablutions courtyard and the prayer hall, with the main entrance in the north wall of the courtyard, facing the mihrab, the niche indicating the direction of Mecca. The arch into which the door was set can still be seen today. Its opulent plasterwork served to emphasize its hallowed status; Moorish geometric motifs decorate the inner surface of the arch, and some fragments survive in the porch. The doors leading to the **Patio de los Naranjos** (Orange Tree Court) are made of bronze-plated wood and decorated with minute Moorish motifs and religious inscriptions in Kufic script. The two splendidly carved bronze door-knockers are replicas; the originals, exceptional examples of Almohad art, are now on display inside the cathedral.

Patio de los Naranjos, aerial view

The main entrance in the north wall of the courtyard, which became known as the Puerta del Perdón (Door of Forgiveness) during the Christian era, underwent a number of renovations but has remained unaltered since the sixteenth century. Between 1519 and 1520, the master craftsman Miguel Perrin made the terracotta relief that shows Christ casting out the Moneylenders, as well as the statues of the Annunciation and of St Peter and St Paul. The plasterwork decoration with plant and animal motifs was carried out later, while the bell gable above the door was not completed until the end of the sixteenth century.

Only one of the entrances to the mosque still serves its original function. This is the Puerta del Lagarto (Lizard Door) next to the former minaret. It is famous for its fine Mozarabic vaulting. This type of vaulting was also used in the porches of the cathedral's other doors, while some fragments are preserved in the rooms now occupied by the world-renowned Columbus Library. The collection, which began with a donation from Alfonso X, known as the Wise, has since increased to more than 90,000 titles. It includes unique volumes dating as far back as the thirteenth century; among these are Pedro de Pamplona's Bible; the Roman Pontifical, a book

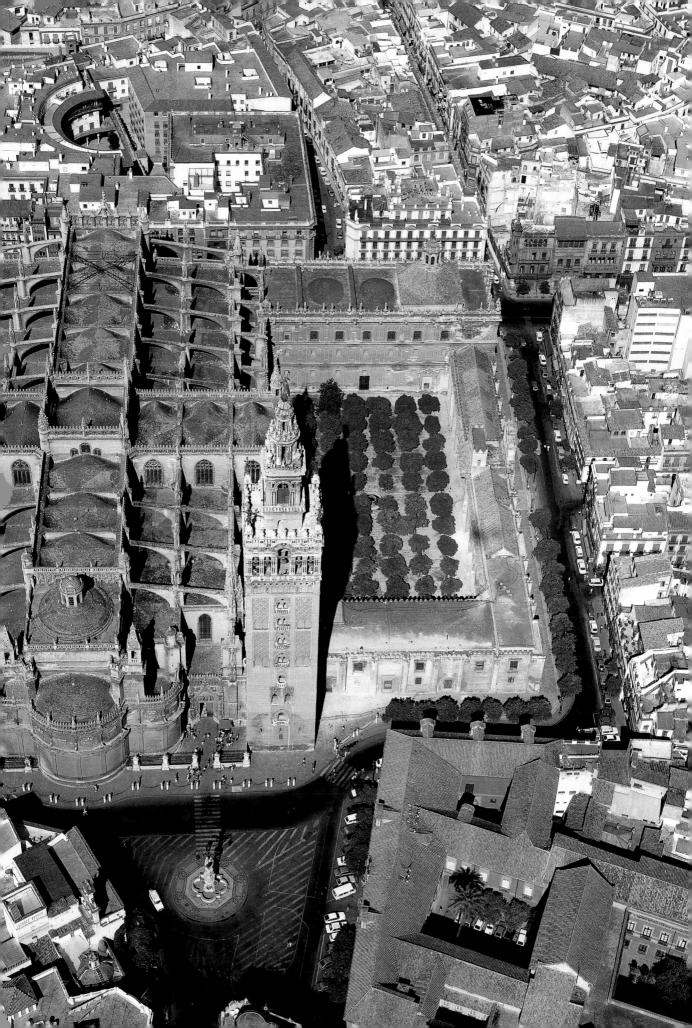

of prayers and instructions for the performance of rituals, begun in 1390 and belonging to the Bishop of Calahorra; the fifteenth-century Carthusian, or Sevillian, Missal; and Queen Isabella the Catholic's *Book of Hours*. Some 20,000 volumes were bequeathed by Don Hernando Colón, on condition that his legacy should be permanently kept together, but not all have survived. Among the most important titles in this bequest are *El Libro de las Profesías*, a book of prophesies compiled by Christopher Columbus for Ferdinand and Isabella, Pierre D'Ailly's *Tractatus de Ymagine Mundi*, published in 1480, and the *Libro de Cosmografía* with annotations by Columbus himself. Such titles are sufficient to indicate the quality and rarity of the treasures that the library contains.

The Patio de los Naranjos remained unaltered until 1618, when the west wing was demolished to make way for the Iglesia del Sagrario (Church of the Sacrament). In the centre of the courtyard, a fountain providing water for ritual ablutions once stood in a small niche; the spot is now occupied by a marble basin of Visigothic origin. Traces of the pillars that once supported the arcade leading to the mosque's

Opposite: Patio de los Naranjos

Right: Puerta del Perdón, door knocker

prayer hall have recently been rediscovered. Construction of the minaret began in 1184, overseen by the architect Ahmad ben Basso, who built a base of stone blocks taken from the neighbouring citadel, as well as pedestals and other pieces recovered from Roman monuments. After a period of inactivity, work was resumed in 1188, under the supervision of Ali al-Gomari, who decided to use bricks instead of stone blocks. Building was completed in March 1198, with the installation of the *yamur*, a gilt bronze finial consisting of four spheres that would sparkle in the sunlight, so that the minaret could be seen for miles around. In common with most other Almohad minarets, the interior consists of several superimposed chambers, each with different types of vaulting. Between the chambers and the outer walls there is a ramp that becomes increasingly narrow but less steep as it continues upwards beneath its vaulted ceiling. The four external walls are each divided into three vertical sections, with panels of *sebqa* (ornate brickwork) on either side of a central section, which contains pairs of window bays. Inside these are elaborate ironwork arches, set within others with serrated edges; the spandrels are decorated with Moorish motifs. Each of the four sides of the minaret is topped by a frieze of interwoven blind arches. The top was originally surmounted by a prism, which formed the base of the *yamur*.

In 1356, when the building was already given over to Christian worship, an earthquake destroyed the *yamur*, and the minaret's appearance was radically altered. The crest was replaced by a small bell gable, which remained until 1558, when work began on the present structure, a belfry designed by Hernán Ruiz the Younger. Architecturally, it was a challenge. Nevertheless, Ruiz found ingenious ways of solving problems of stability and resistance, while at the same time displaying his great talent for design. The belfry, which combines ashlar, bricks and glazed tiles, comprises five superimposed storeys of diminishing size, popularly known as the

Below: Puerta del Lagarto, Mozarabic vaulting

Opposite: Miguel Perrín, *Christ Casts out the Moneylenders from the Temple* (1519-22), Puerta del Perdón

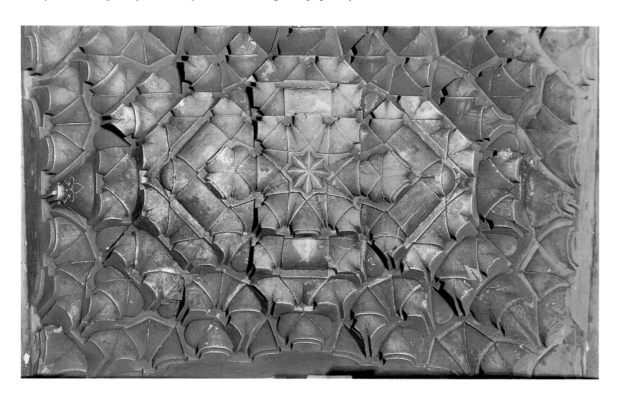

Bells, the Clock, the Stars (or the Well), the Billiard Balls (or Round sections), and the Crest. It is crowned by a monumental bronze statue of Faith Triumphant, popularly known as El Giraldillo, which also serves as a weathervane. The statue appears to have been based on an engraving of Pallas Athene by Marcantonio Raimondi, from an original likeness by Giulio Romano or Perina del Vaga. The design is attributed to Luis de Vargas, while the mould was made by the sculptor Juan Bautista Vázquez the Elder and the bronze cast by Bartolomé Morel. Also attributed to Morel are the male busts, which may have been intended to represent the Prophets, and the faun-like masks and images of cherubim that adorn the whole structure. Building work, which lasted ten years, also affected the original tower, which was renovated so that it should harmonize, both aesthetically and in terms of colour, with the new belfry. The walls were painted, balconies were added to the windows, and discs of glazed tiling set into the walls. Luis de Vargas also painted a series of frescoes of Seville's patron saints, the Apostles, the Evangelists and the Doctors of the Church, which have not survived. Along with the colossal statue of Faith Triumphant, such images, placed at strategic points of the tower, together constitute a declaration in favour of the Counter Reformation, proclaiming the triumph of the Catholic Faith and the Church of Rome.

The Giralda

Luis de Vargas, Juan Bautista Vázquez and Bartolomé Morel, Giraldillo, detail (1566-68)

It was after the conquest of Seville by Ferdinand III in 1248 that the Almohad mosque was adapted for Christian worship. The direction of the nave and aisles was established along an east–west axis and the building was consecrated as the Cathedral Church of Santa María. There were various alterations, additions and repairs, but no substantial change was made to the appearance of the building until the fifteenth century.

The Gothic Cathedral

By 1401, the building had become so dilapidated that it was decided to tear it down and replace it with a new stone-built cathedral in the Gothic style. The precise date at which work began on the new building is unknown, but it is highly unlikely that this was before 1433, when Juan II authorized the demolition of the Royal Chapel in the old cathedral. The construction of the new cathedral began at the west end, possibly at the north-western corner, but there is no record of who drew up the plans. Nevertheless, the important role played by the master builder Carlín in the initial stages is well documented, and Isambret is known to have been on site at some stage. Later on, works were overseen successively by Juan Norman, Juan de Hoces, Simón de Colonia, Alonso Rodríguez and Juan Gil de Hontañón.

Seville Cathedral, the largest Gothic church in world, is built on a rectangular ground plan. The nave is flanked by two aisles, with chapels leading off between the buttresses. The nave and the transept are wider and higher than the aisles. There is no ambulatory; instead a rectangular passage separates the Capilla Mayor (Main Chapel), beyond the crossing, from the Capilla Real (Royal Chapel), in the apse. The west front is pierced by three doors; there are also two doors into the high altar, a door at each arm of the crossing and on each side of the apse. The tall, slender pillars, set on polygonal bases, are composed of fine vertical mouldings, resembling bunches of reeds, some of which extend into the austere cross vaulting above the nave. These are in sharp contrast to the magnificent fan vaulting, typical of the late Gothic style, above the crossing and the chapels.

View of the side aisles

A narrow clerestory-like gallery runs above the central nave and the transept, and continues over the chapels between the crossing and the high altar. The richly decorated parapet is divided by small pinnacled columns.

While little is known about the initial stages of the cathedral's construction, the building process was more fully documented from the mid-fifteenth century, so that it is possible to date the various sections of the cathedral. For example, by 1449, work was well advanced on the chapels between the main façade and the transept and the small doorways leading

Cathedral exterior

Opposite: South transept

into them. Around 1467, under the supervision of Juan Norman, the side aisles were built, with the exception of those nearest the high altar. Eleven years later, the nave from the main door to the transept was virtually finished. In 1481, Juan de Hoces completed the two doorways in the high altar and, during the following decade, work continued on the vaulting closest to the high altar. In 1506, Alonso Rodríguez laid the last stone in the main dome, and parapets for various sections were completed four years later. Swift progress promised a rapid end to construction, but in 1511 the main dome and the neighbouring vaults caved in.

This unfortunate accident destroyed not only several sections of vaulting and the slender spire above the transept but also some beautiful multicoloured tiling by Francisco Niculoso Pisano and several terracotta figures by Jorge Fernández and Pedro Millán. As planners considered the construction of a new dome, proposals were made to cover it with a wooden frame in the Mudéjar style. The idea was finally rejected but, had it been accepted, it would have completely changed the appearance of Seville Cathedral. The new dome, designed by Juan Gil de Hontañón, was lower and simpler, although it was decorated with several terracotta images by Miguel Perrin. The new vaults over the transept were completed in 1517, the ones above the choir having been completed two years earlier. The main dome and some of the vaults collapsed in 1888, and were rebuilt under the supervision of Joaquín Fernández Ayarragaray.

Of the doorways in the cathedral's west front, only the smaller ones leading to the side aisles date from the fifteenth century. That on the left is known as the Puerta del Bautistero (Baptistry Door) and that on the right the Puerta del Nacimiento (Nativity Door), named after the scenes of the Baptism and Birth of Christ depicted on their respective tympanums. The Puerta del Nacimiento is also called the Puerta de San Miguel, after the cathedral school of the same name that stood nearby. Both are decorated with terracotta figures, most of which are of outstanding quality. In the Puerta del Bautistero the tympanum is filled by figures of Christ, St John the Baptist and an angel, while angels and Prophets occupy the door surrounds, and Seville's own patron saints, Justa, Fulgentius, Isidore, Leander, Florentina and Rufina, stand in the open niches on either side of the door. Apart from the figures of the Prophets, which are attributed to Pedro Millán, they are all believed to be the work of Lorenzo Mercadante de Bretaña dating from 1464. In the Puerta del Nacimiento, the Nativity scene, protected by Gothic canopies, includes a female figure, the Angel appearing to the Shepherds, and an urban landscape, supposedly representing the town of Bethlehem. At the base of the door surround are various images of the Prophets, and the rest of the surround is occupied by angels playing musical instruments. The large sculptures on the door frame represent St Laureano (one of Seville's first archbishops), St Mark and St John on the left, and St Matthew, St Luke and St Hermenegild (another Sevillian martyr) on the right. The figures in the tympanum and surrounding the door are by Lorenzo Mercadante de Bretaña, while the Prophets are by Pedro Millán. These figures by Mercadante are among the finest examples of medieval sculpture; they reflect the Burgundian style of the period but with a sense of realism reminiscent of Flemish portraiture.

The main door, the Puerta de la Asunción (Assumption Door), was not completed until the nineteenth century. At the request of Cardinal Cienfuegos y Jovellanos, Fernando Rosales worked on the door from 1829 until 1831, his scheme being in keeping with the predominantly Gothic style of the building. Before the sculptural decoration was even started, work on the door was halted and did not resume until 1877, when Joaquín Fernández took over. In 1882, responsibility for the decoration passed to Ricardo Bellver, who began with the large relief of the Assumption in the tympanum. Three years later, Bellver started work on the eighty figures that were to occupy the various sections of the doorway. But he never completed the series and he delivered the last statues in 1899. Both the reliefs and the statues were carved from reconstituted stone, provoking criticism among some of the city's intellectuals.

The great doors at each end of the transept were also completed not in the Middle Ages but in the nineteenth century. Both are by Adolfo Fernández Casanova, whose design echoes the existing Gothic elements of the building. Basing his work on plans drawn up by Demetrio de los Ríos in 1866, he put into practice the French theory that architects should respect the original style of a building when restoring or adding to it. The door on the south side (1887-95) is known as the Puerta de San Cristóbal (St Christopher's Door). It is also called Puerta de la Lonja, because it faces the Lonja, the old stock exchange. Yet another name is the Puerta del Príncipe (Prince's Door), because it is the entrance used by members of the royal family. The door on the north side (1895-1927), which opens

Capilla Real, vaulting

onto the Patio de los Naranjos, has decorative carvings by Joaquín Bilbao, Adolfo López and Eduardo Muñoz.

The apse of Seville Cathedral is pierced by two doors. This unusual feature can be explained by the need to provide access between the cathedral and the Corral de los Olmos (Elm Tree Court), where the cathedral chapter and other offices were initially based. The two doors, known respectively as the Puerta de los Palos, after the *palos* (fence posts) that once stood nearby, and the Puerta de las Campanillas, after the bells that once summoned the cathedral craftsmen to work. The first is decorated by a scene of the Adoration of the Magi, with figures of angels, and the second by the Entry into Jerusalem, with figures of the Prophets. The reliefs in each tympanum and the free-standing sculptures were executed by Miguel Perrin from 1520 onwards.

The two doors in the apse stand on either side of the Capilla Real (Royal Chapel), whose circular walls are divided by two tiers of superimposed pilasters; those in the lower tier are Corinthian and appear to be suspended on corbels, and those in the upper tier are Ionic. In between are various royal and imperial coats of arms. The main dome is surrounded by a balustrade above the cornice. Supported by buttresses in the angles of the dome are some of the original niches. Building was

Opposite: Maestre Carlín. Puerta
del Bautismo (ca. 1450)

Right: Lorenzo Mercadante de
Bretaña, St Rufina (1464-67),
Puerta del Bautismo

Above: Lorenzo Mercadante de Bretaña, Nativity (ca. 1460), Puerta del Nacimiento

Left: Puerta del Nacimiento or de San Miguel (ca. 1460)

Opposite: Fernando Rosales, Joaquín Fernández and Ricardo Bellver (1829-83), Puerta de la Asunción

Page 26: Miguel Perrín, The Entry into Jerusalem (1522), Puerta de Campanillas

Page 27 above: Exterior view of the south wall and the Boveda de la Sacristia

Page 27 below: Façade of the Capilla Real, Plaza Virgen de los Reyes

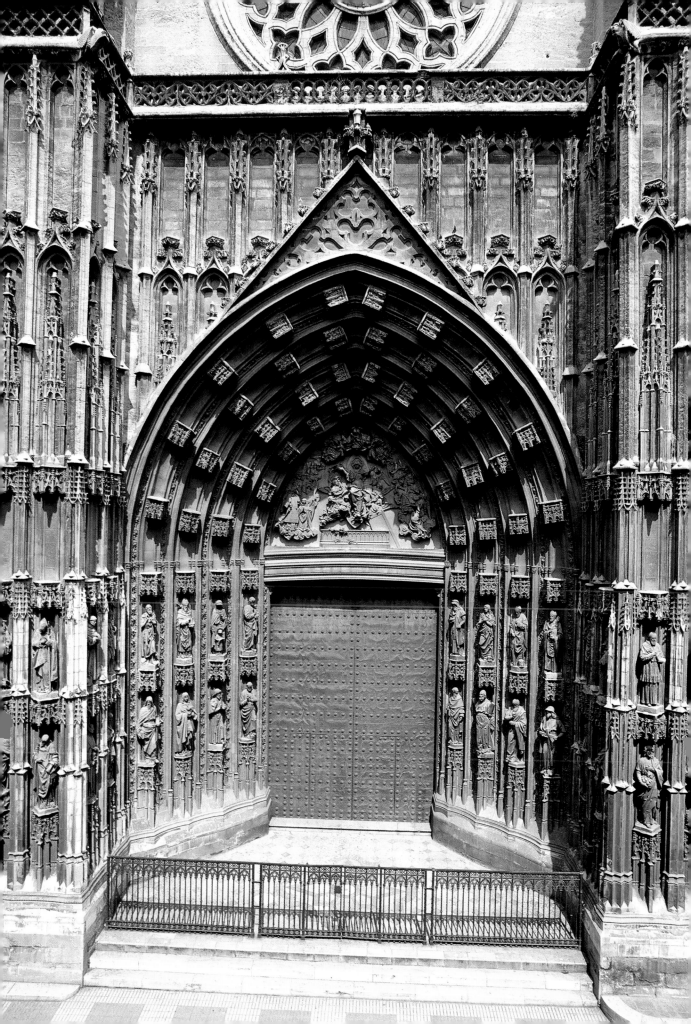

started in 1551 by Martin de Gainza, and Hernán Ruiz the Younger later took over the construction of the domes and the niches.

Adjoining the south-eastern wall of the cathedral, between the Puerta de las Campanillas at the east end and the Puerta de San Cristóbal in the south side, are extensions to the cathedral added during the sixteenth century. These include the Sacristía Mayor (Main Sacristy) and the Sacristía de los Cálices (Sacristy of the Chalices), the chapterhouse and the counting house. The wall that encloses them, begun by Diego de Riaño in 1529, was not completed until the final decades of the century, at the same time as the other additions. The wall is divided by a series of massive pilasters set on pedestals and topped by a balustrade of torch holders. Medallions, one of which contains a portrait of Hercules, are set into the upper parts of some sections of the wall. The various rooms behind the wall are lit by a row of windows. The four largest were designed by Asensio de Maeda, while the railings (1594-96) are the work of Rodrigo de Segovia. The corridor window, which leads into the chapterhouse and is set into the eastern wall between those of the counting house and chapterhouse itself, is the only one with ornamental reliefs. It was built by Hernán Ruiz the Younger in 1561.

In the eighteenth century, further extensions to the cathedral became necessary and a new wall had to be erected between the Puerta de San Cristóbal and Capilla de San Laureano (Chapel of St Laureano), at the south-western extremity of the cathedral. Although it was built in the style of the sixteenth-century wall, it was not as monumental. Work began in 1758, to plans by José de Herrera, but this was interrupted a few years later and did not resume until 1793. After various problems and changes to the plans, the wall was eventually completed by Francisco Javier de Luque in 1929.

An integral part of Seville Cathedral is its magnificent stained-glass windows, which in terms of space, iconography and meaning, define the whole concept of this imposing Gothic building. The design and positioning of the windows depended heavily on the building process, especially the closing off of the vaults. Because they were designed and installed at different times, they do not follow a consistent formal arrangement, although they are harmonious in terms of their subject matter. While the windows designed by Enrique Alemán are Alsatian in shape and Flemish in influence, those by Juan Jacques follow the French style prevalent around 1500, and those by Arnao de Vergara, Arnao de Flandes, Carlos de Brujas and Vicente Menardo are based on Renaissance and Mannerist ideas, which were novel at the time.

The windows are arranged in such a way as to illustrate specific themes; each portrays the various episodes of a story in pictures, although architectural requirements sometimes took precedence over pictorial content. Since the first part of the cathedral to be built was the west front, the first windows to be installed were those lighting the aisles and nave. Most were made by Enrique Alemán between 1478 and 1483. Those lighting the nave contain representations of the Prophets in a cycle. They form a sequence with the Four Evangelists in the rose window in the west front, indicating that the latter relied on the writings of their predecessors. Representations of saints, apostles, martyrs and Doctors of the Church are featured in the transept windows and in those that light the side aisles in the space that extends from the east end to the transept. Enrique Alemán began this

Opposite: Carlos de Brujas,
The Resurrection (1558)

Page 30: Juan Jacques,
The Glorification of the Virgin
(1511-20)

Page 31 left: Arnao de Vergara,
St Sebastian (1535)

Page 31 right: Enrique Alemán,
The Four Evangelists (1478)

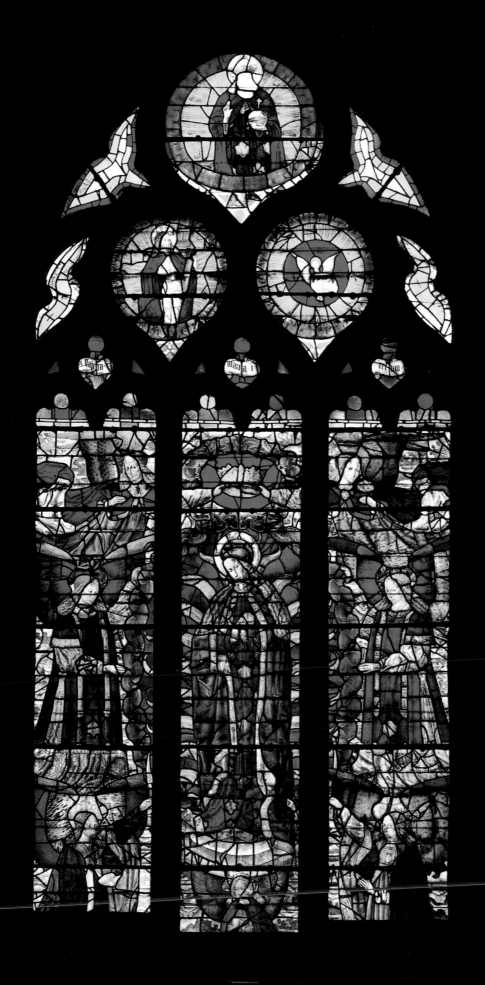

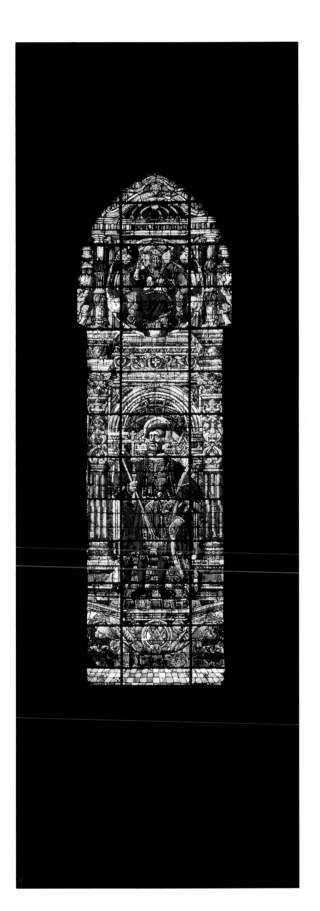
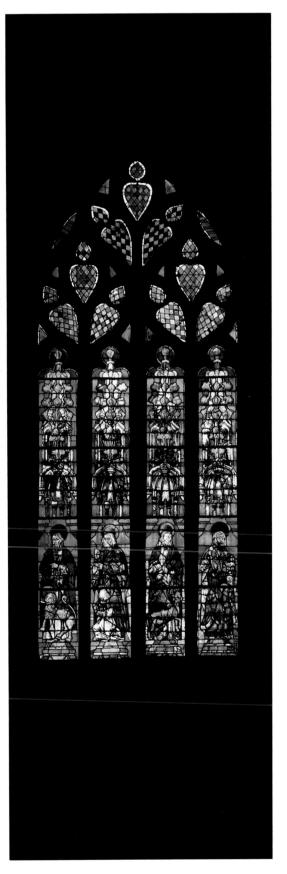

series, but Arnao de Flandes completed it between 1543 and 1552. Although these windows show conceptual differences, they are linked to the ones above the Puerta de Palos and the Puerta de Campanillas, which show St Sebastian and St Christopher. This same series of windows provides the thematic basis for those made for the sanctuary in the early sixteenth century by Juan Jacques, and for those depicting scenes from the life of the Virgin Mary, made by Arnao de Vergara for the dome. These in turn were the starting point for the imagery in the windows of the aisles, which are set in the wall between the transept and the high altar. The majority of them were made by Arnao de Flandes between 1553 and 1556 and show scenes from the life of Christ. The rest of the stained-glass windows were made in 1913 by F. X. Zettler, the Munich-based company, or were reconstructed following the collapse of the dome.

Just as the windows of the nave and aisle illustrate specific themes, so those in the chapels are intended to tell a variety of stories. The subjects depicted in these single windows were usually chosen to reflect the name of the chapel. Some of them date from the sixteenth century and are the work of the same artists responsible for the main cycle. Others were made in the seventeenth and eighteenth centuries, and there are some of nineteenth-century origin, which represent a period in which the glazier's art underwent a complete reappraisal. The last windows to be installed in the chapels date from between 1929 and 1934, coinciding with the restoration of all the cathedral's stained-glass windows.

Capilla Mayor

The Capilla Mayor (Main Chapel) is fronted by three gilt *rejas* (altar screens) in the High Renaissance style. The central *reja* (1518-29) was made by the Dominican friar Francisco de Salamanca; it consists of four horizontal sections and four vertical divisions. In the lower tracery frieze angels flank a profile bust of Christ. The upper frieze and cresting contain images of the Prophets and a central scene of the Entombment. The pulpits (1527-32) on either side of the central *reja* are also the work of Francisco de Salamanca; that on the left bears representations of the Four Evangelists and that on the right shows scenes from the life of St Paul.

The two side *rejas* are of similar design to the central one, though they are decorated with floral and plant motifs. They were started by the *rejero* (craftsman specializing in *rejas*) Sancho Muñoz in 1518 and completed in 1522 by Diego Huidobro and Juan de Cubillana.

The great altarpiece (1482-1564) behind the altar of the Capilla Mayor is the focal point of the cathedral. It is one of the finest of its kind and is the work of several craftsmen, most notably Pierre Dancart, who designed it and worked on it

Below, left: Bartolomé de Jaén and Fray Francisco de Salamanca. Main *reja* (1518-29)

Below, right: Capilla Mayor, general view

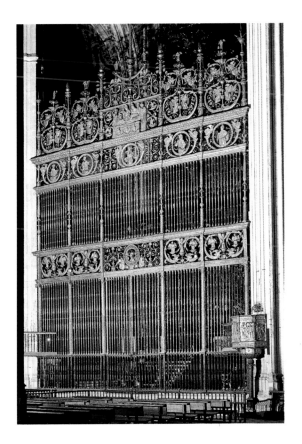

Opposite: The Virgin of the See
(thirteenth century), Altarpiece
of the Capilla Mayor

Top: Jorge and Alejo Fernández
Alemán, Christ in Agony,
Altarpiece of the Capilla Mayor

Above: Jorge and Alejo
Fernández Alemán, Roque
Balduque, and Juan Bautista
Vázquez the Elder *et al*
(fifteenth and sixteenth
centuries), Altarpiece of the
Capilla Mayor

Right: Jorge Fernández,
View of Seville (1508-18),
Altarpiece of the Capilla Mayor

until his death. He was succeeded in turn by Master Marco, Pedro Millán and Jorge and Alejo Fernández Alemán, who completed the central section of the altarpiece in 1560. The two side panels (1560-64) are by Roque Balduque, Juan Batista Vázquez the Elder and Pedro Heredia.

The altarpiece contains forty-four reliefs, with numerous sculptures adorning the dividing pilasters. It is crowned by a canopy decorated with octagonal caissons. Above it is a beam, carved by Jorge Fernández and polychromed by his brother, with a Pietà and the Twelve Apostles. The centrepiece is a fourteenth-century Gothic crucifix, whose figure of the Crucified Christ is popularly known as the Christ of the Million. The reliefs on the predella (panel at the base of the altarpiece) show the martyrdom of various saints, but there are also some interesting views of Seville in the scenes that involve the city's patron saints: Justa and Rufina, Leander and Isidore. In the centre is the Gothic statue of the Virgin of the See, which shows French influences and is thought to date from the thirteenth century. It is carved in wood and covered with silver plate.

The scenes represented on the first (lowest) section of the altarpiece show the Embrace of St Joachim and St Ann, the Birth of the Virgin, the Annunciation, the Nativity, the Slaughter of the Innocents, the Circumcision and the Adoration of the Magi. The second section illustrates the Presentation of Jesus in the Temple, the Baptism of Christ, the Raising of Lazarus, the Assumption, Christ's Entry into Jerusalem, the Last Supper and Christ's Agony in the Garden. The third section shows Christ taken before Pilate, the Scourging of Christ, the Resurrection, the Ecce Homo, the Passion, and Christ Stripped of his Garments. The fourth (uppermost) section shows the Burial of Christ, the Three Marys at the Sepulchre, Mary Magdalene with the Risen Christ, the Ascension, Christ's Descent into Limbo, the Supper at Emmaus and the Pentecost.

The side screen on the left of the altarpiece shows, from bottom to top, the Creation of Eve, the Flight into Egypt, Christ among the Doctors, the

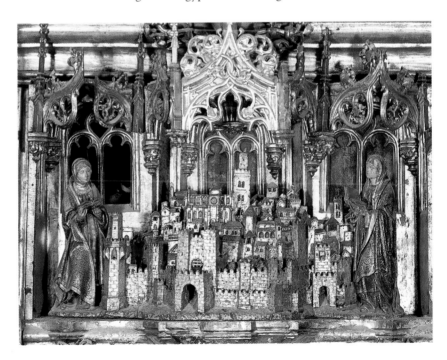

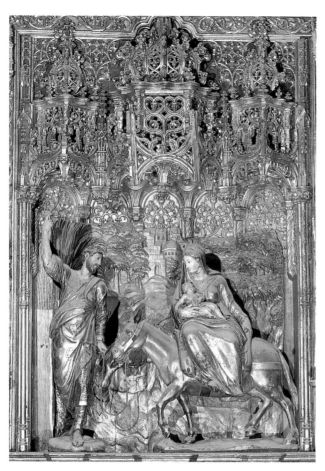

Left: Roque Balduque and Juan
Bautista Vázquez, The Flight
into Egypt (ca. 1560), Altarpiece
of the Capilla Mayor

Below: Juan Bautista Vázquez,
Original Sin (1563), Altarpiece of
the Capilla Mayor

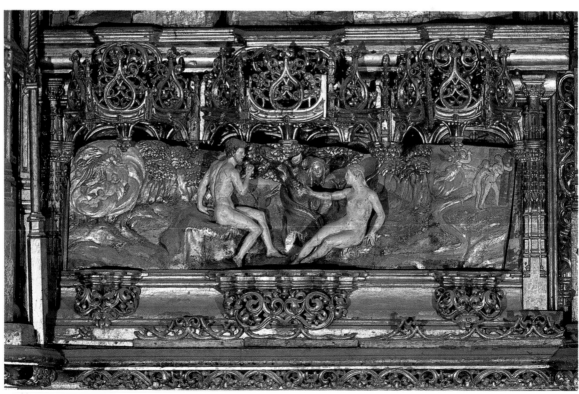

Transfiguration, and Mary Magdalene anointing Christ. The side screen on the right shows the Fall of Adam and Eve, the Last Judgement, the Miracle of the Loaves and the Fishes, Christ Casting out the Moneylenders, and the Conversion of St Paul. The columns are covered with images of the Kings of Judah. On the altar table is an oval silver-gilt tabernacle (1593-98) by Francisco de Alfaro, which features barley-sugar columns (also known as Solomonic columns because they were presumed to imitate those in the temple in Jerusalem). A pair of lecterns (1594-96), also by Francisco de Alfaro, flank the altar. Other interesting pieces of silverwork are the altar frontal (1739) by Manuel Guerrero de Alcántara and the life-size statues of St Leander and St Isidore (probably 1741, with later restoration); they are carved in wood, their clothing overlaid with silver and incrusted with precious stones.

Above: Francisco de Alfaro, Tabernacle (1593-96), Altarpiece of the Capilla Mayor

Below: Manuel Guerrero de Alcántara, High Altar Frontal (1739)

When special ceremonies were performed at the high altar, the altar frontal and the statues were put together so as to create a silver throne, or altar table. The altar itself was begun in 1688 by Juan Laureano de Pina, and completed by Manuel Guerrero. It was refurbished between 1770 and 1772. It is now used for Maundy Thursday ceremonies, when it is placed at the foot of the nave.

A high wall encloses the sides and rear of the Capilla Mayor and separates it from the Sacristía Alta (High Sacristy). This space, completed in about 1520, has a

coffered ceiling in the Renaissance style and each of the octagonal and square caissons has a pine cone in the centre. The windows also date from the mid-sixteenth century. The free-standing statues of saints, kings, prophets, bishops and martyrs on the upper part of the wall are by various hands, including Miguel Perrin, Juan Martín and Diego Pesquera. The most striking, and the only one that is painted, is the statue of the Virgin of Repose, attributed to Miguel Perrin, which adorns the front wall of the Capilla Real, flanked by the patron saints of Seville.

In the centre of this wall, beneath the windows of the Sacristía Alta, hang two great Baroque canvases: *The Soldiers of Gideon*, by an unknown seventeenth-century painter, and *The Marriage of Joseph and Mary* (1657) by Valdés Leal. Below is the entrance to the Capilla de Nuestra Señora del Solterrano (Chapel of our Lady of the Undercroft), endowed by the Marquess and Marchioness of Yanduri. The chapel's altarpiece (1925), representing the Holy Family, the Pietà and a man at prayer, is by Mariano Benlliure.

Above: Cayetano de Acosta and Fernando de Cáceres, St Isidore (eighteenth century), restored in 1772

Above, left: Miguel Perrín, The Virgin of Repose (ca. 1540), Retrochoir

Portals of the choir

The portals on each side of the choir were begun in 1725, and are the cathedral's main eighteenth-century architectural component. They were needed to provide a base that was both sufficiently sturdy and aesthetically pleasing to support the cases of the new organs. Two sets of plans were drawn up by Archbishop Diego Díaz's official architect and the most sumptuous of the two was chosen. No expense was spared on these portals, which consist of a combination of red and black marble and gilt bronze. Each portal has two doors, one real and the other false. The real doors are made of ebony, and the false ones of jasper. All four are inlaid with polished copper plate; they bear the signature of the sculptor Luis de Vilches and are dated 1730. The project was completed in 1732.

Above the portals rise the colossal organs. The cases are by Luis de Vilches and Pedro Duque Cornejo, who worked on them for seven years, starting in 1724. Standing on tribunes supported by a statue of Atlas, aided by a number of children, and topped with exuberant angels playing musical instruments, they are remarkable pieces of Baroque sculpture. The organ case opposite the Capilla de la Virgen de la Antigua had to be rebuilt after it was severely damaged when the dome collapsed in 1888. At the end of the nineteenth century, soon after having undergone major modifications to extend their range of expression, the original Baroque-period instruments were replaced by Aquilino Amezua.

Right: Portico and organ of the Capilla de la Virgen de la Antigua

Overleaf: Capillas de los Albastros, de la Encarnación and de la Inmaculada Concepción

Hernán Ruiz the Younger,
Cosme de Sorribes and Pedro
Delgado, Capilla de la Virgen
de la Estrella (1568)

Las Capillas de los Alabastros

Immediately to the south of the portals are the four Capillas de los Alabastros (Alabaster Chapels), which take their name from the alabaster of which they are built. The two chapels on the south side, off the aisle of St Paul, are dedicated respectively to the Immaculate Conception and the Incarnation. They are in the Gothic style and were begun in 1515 by Juan Gil de Hontañón. The two chapels on the north side, off the aisle of St Peter, are dedicated respectively to the Virgin of the Star and St Gregory. They are in the Renaissance style and are by Diego de Riaño, who began work on them in 1529. The pillars framing the latter two chapels are set with ten small Gothic figures of the Apostles, installed during the first stage of building. The twelve statues of female saints adorning the inner surfaces of the entrance arches were carved in 1531 by Nicolás de León, at the same time as Riaño was working on the vaults.

Capilla de San Gregorio

The Capilla de San Gregorio (Chapel of St Gregory) is closed off by a *reja* built by Marcos de la Cruz in 1650. It is a copy of the *reja* in the neighbouring Capilla de la Virgen de la Estrella. The statue of St Gregory is by Manuel García de Santiago and dates from the mid-eighteenth century.

Capilla de la Virgen de la Estrella

This burial chapel, dedicated to the Virgin of the Star, was built in 1566 for Rodrigo Franco and his descendants. The *reja* was designed by Hernán Ruiz the Younger and Cosme de Sorribas and built by the *rejero* Pedro Delgado. It is dated 1568 and features a variety of Plateresque ornamentation, of which the most notable pieces include the figures of the Virtues above the door and the medallions and angels in the cresting. The focal point of the chapel is an eighteenth-century Baroque altarpiece decorated with Rococo motifs, mirrors and silverwork. The statue of the Virgin of the Star that stands in the vaulted niche dates from the sixteenth century but was retouched and repainted in the second half of the eighteenth.

The Retrochoir

The original plans for the jasper retrochoir, decorated with marble sculptures and reliefs and with gilt bronze busts, were drawn up by Miguel de Zumárraga in 1619. When it was first built, it aroused an intense and long-lasting controversy among some of Seville's most prestigious contemporary artists. It was finally decided to suspend work and dismantle part of the finished structure. The debate was rekindled and the decision made to build the retrochoir using materials from the original project. The cathedral's works superintendent at the time was the architect Pedro Sánchez Falconete, who is believed to be responsible for the final design.

The retrochoir is organized around the focal point, a painting of the Virgen de los Remedios (Our Lady of Succour), which dates from around 1400. On either side are pedimented doorways, which provide access to the choir and the organ lofts. The wall is embellished with a number of sculptures and reliefs depicting biblical

themes; these date from different periods and were executed in different materials. There are also the coats-of-arms of the cathedral chapter, busts of St Justa and St Rufina, and a painting on copper by Francisco Pacheco (1634) of Ferdinand III receiving the keys of the city. In 1635, Juan Sánchez began work on the *reja* separating the retrochoir from the nave; this was the final stage of the revised scheme.

Above: Miguel de Zumárraga and Pedro Sánchez Falconete, Retrochoir (1619-35)

Opposite: Juan Martínez Montañés, La Cieguecita, (1628-31) Capilla de la Inmaculada Concepción

Capilla de la Inmaculada Concepción

The *reja* of the Capilla de la Inmaculada Concepción (Chapel of the Immaculate Conception) dates from the second quarter of the seventeenth century and is yet another copy of that in the Capilla de la Virgen de la Estrella.

The statue of the Immaculate Conception (1628-31) that forms the focal point of the altarpiece is by Juan Martínez Montañes. Because of her downcast gaze, which reinforces her attitude of humility, the Virgin represented by this statue is popularly known as La Cieguecita (Little Blind One). Flanking it on the altarpiece are smaller statues of St Gregory and St John the Baptist, and reliefs of St Jerome, St Francis, St Joseph and St Joachim.

Portraits of the chapel's donors, Don Francisco Gutiérrez de Molina and Doña Jerónima Zamudio, by Francisco Pacheco, are set into the predella. The decoratively tiled altar frontal was designed by José Gestoso in 1908 and made by the potter Manual Amores.

Capilla de la Encarnación

The Capilla de la Encarnación (Chapel of the Incarnation) was founded by Don Juan Serón and Doña Antonia de Verástegui. The *reja*, made in the mid-seventeenth century, is a copy of the one in the Chapel of the Virgin of the Star, which dates from the sixteenth century. The predella of the seventeenth-century altarpiece bears reliefs of the busts of various saints, with a central scene showing the moment of

Incarnation, and an image of God, the Eternal Father, on the cresting. The inscription in silver lettering on the canopy alludes to the name of the chapel. The glazed tile altar frontal was designed by José Gestoso, and made by Manuel Ramos in 1909 in the pottery workshops of Seville's Triana district.

On the pillar between this chapel and the adjoining one stands an alabaster statue of the Virgin of Genoa. It dates from the second half of the fourteenth century and its style is reminiscent of works produced in the studio of Nino Pisano. The figure once belonged to the Genoese brotherhood in Seville and was transferred here from the Church of St Sebastian.

Choir

The choir is fronted by one of Seville Cathedral's most beautiful *rejas*. It is made of gilt wrought iron, and was designed by Sancho Muñoz and made by Fray Francisco de Salamanca between 1518 and 1523. Although it was severely damaged when the dome collapsed, craftsmen working under the direction of José Gestoso restored it to its original state. The *reja* consists of a podium and two sections, with frieze and crest. The frieze contains images of St Peter, St Paul, St Andrew and St James the Great of Compostela. The crest incorporates the Tree of Jesse, showing the genealogy of Christ, including not only the Virgin and the Christ Child but also images of biblical patriarchs and kings.

The choir contains seating for 117 choristers, sixty-seven in the upper stalls and fifty in the lower. Most of the choir stalls are made of ebony. The lower stalls are decorated with small Gothic arches and the misericords depict creatures from the medieval bestiary. On the backs are representations of the Giralda as it was in the

Below: Sancho Muñoz and Fray Francisco de Salamanca, Choir *reja* (1518-23)

Opposite, above: Nufro Sánchez, Dancart, Gómez de Horozco and Juan Alemán *et al.*. Choir stalls (1470-1520)

Opposite, below: Upper choir stalls (1470-1520)

fifteenth century, while the headrests are adorned with reliefs of scenes from the Old and New Testaments. The upper stalls are of similar design, but the backs are decorated with Mudéjar motifs. They are framed by pointed arches and the mouldings between the stalls are delicately carved. Above them runs a pierced canopy with small sculptures. The stall reserved for the king – the second on the upper row – is inlaid with the coats-of-arms of Castile and León, and bears the inscription '*Este coro fizo Nufro Sánchez que Dios aya acabose año 1478*' ('Nufro Sánchez sculptor made this choir, finished by the grace of God in the year 1478'). The choir's Mudéjar features are the work of Sánchez. Its Gothic elements, dating from 1479, were probably fashioned by the northern European master craftsman Pierre Dancart. During the sixteenth century, Gonzálo Gómez and Horozco and Diego Guillén also worked on the choir stalls.

The archbishop's throne is flanked by two paintings, one of the Immaculate Conception, painted by Francisco Pacheco in about 1620, the other a Crucifixion from the studio of Zurbarán. In the centre of the choir is a wooden and bronze lectern (1562-65) designed by Hernán Ruiz the Younger and made by the sculptors Juan Marín, Francisco Hernández and Juan Bautista Vázquez. The lectern consists of a circular base supporting a truncated pyramid, both decorated with reliefs. It is topped by a Madonna and Child, crowned in turn by a Crucifix surrounded by the Four Evangelists. These sculptures are by Juan Bautista Vázquez, while the bronze elements of the lectern were cast by Bartolomé Morel.

Above, left: Hernán Ruiz the Younger, Juan Marín and Juan Bautista Vázquez, choir lectern (1562-65)

Above: Francisco Pacheco, *Immaculate Conception* (ca. 1620), choir

Northern Chapels

Capilla de la Virgen del Pilar

Since it forms an integral part of the porch of the Patio de los Naranjos, the Capilla de la Virgen del Pilar (Chapel of the Virgin of El Pilar) is smaller than the others that line the northern and southern aisles of the cathedral. The chapel takes its name from the former church founded by the Aragonese knights who accompanied Ferdinand III when he reconquered Seville. In the early sixteenth century, it passed to the Pinelo family of Genoa, who used it as a family burial chapel. Their coats of arms can be seen near the *reja*, which dates from 1717. Above is a stained-glass window (1553) depicting Christ's Entry into Jerusalem, by Arnao de Flandes.

The chapel's altarpiece is in the Baroque style and dates from the late seventeenth century. The statue of the Virgin of El Pilar at the centre is by Pedro Millán, who is believed to have completed the work in about 1500. It is made of painted terracotta, and is considered to be Millán's masterpiece. On each side stand statues of St Peter and St Paul, which also probably date from the seventeenth century.

The Baroque altarpiece to the side dates almost certainly from the late seventeenth century. The niche contains a seventeenth-century a statue of St Sebastian flanked by statues of St Inés and St Anthony of Padua.

Pedro Millán, The Virgin of El Pilar (ca. 1500), Capilla de la Virgen del Pilar

Capilla de los Evangelistas

The stained-glass window (1553) depicting the Nativity is the work of Arnao de Flandes, who was also responsible for the one on the outer wall showing the Raising of Lazarus.

The donor of the Capilla de los Evangelistas (Chapel of the Evangelists) was Don Rodrigo de Santillán, Archdeacon of Écija, who commissioned the altarpiece and the paintings by Hernando de Esturmio, a Dutch artist who worked in Seville from 1539 onwards. They depict the Four Evangelists, St Gregory's Mass, and the Resurrection. The predella shows St Catherine with St Barbara, St Sebastian with St John the Baptist and St Antonio Abbot, and Justa and Rufina, two of Seville's patron saints. Between these two is an interesting representation of the Giralda as it appeared before the addition of the present belfry.

The paintings opposite the altar, of St Agnes, St Peter and St John the Baptist, are by Diego Vidal de Liendo the Younger, a painter who was also a prebendary of the cathedral. They were executed during the second quarter of the seventeenth century for two small altarpieces in the Sacristía Mayor and are all copies of pieces by Andrea del Sarto.

The paintings of the Four Evangelists on the wall facing the *reja* are seventeenth-century copies of French engravings. The *Martyrdom of St Peter of Arbues*, attributed to the nineteenth-century painter Joaquín Cortés, is a copy after Murillo.

Capilla de las Doncellas

The Capilla de las Doncellas (Chapel of the Maidens) is fronted by one of the cathedral's most interesting Renaissance *rejas*. It is by Pedro Delgado, and bears the date of its construction and installation (1579). The crest of the *reja* features outstanding metalwork, including a circular relief of the Virgin as Mater Misericordiae (Mother of Mercy).

The stained-glass window (1534) that lights the chapel is by Arnao de Vergara and shows Our Lady of Mercy, protector of young maidens. The upper section

features the Annunciation. This is the emblem of the Brotherhood of Maidens, whose purpose was to provide dowries for impecunious young women. The brotherhood gained possession of the chapel when it was granted to Micer García de Gibraleón, a senior official in the household of Pope Leo X and a member of the brotherhood.

The chapel's altarpiece, which replaces an earlier one installed at the time that the chapel was built, was made by José Rivera in 1771, with gilding, executed in 1775, by Fernando de Cáceres. Large columns divide the predella and central section vertically into three parts. The central section is occupied by a sculptural group representing the Annunciation, and date from the same period. The other paintings belong to the original altarpiece; they are attributed to Cristóbal de Morales, and are believed to date from about 1534. Those flanking the Annunciation group depict St James the Less and St Thomas, and St Bartholomew and St Peter. Those on the predella portray the Fathers of the Church, young women receiving their dowries and the donor of the altarpiece with his coat-of-arms.

The scene of the Crucifixion on the crest was also made for the original altarpiece. The panels of decorative Sevillian tiles at the foot of the altarpiece show the coats-of-arms of the donor. The wrought-iron railing that fronts the altar dates from the early sixteenth century.

Above: Cristóbal de Morales, *Presentation of the Dowries*, Capilla de las Doncellas

Opposite: Glazed-tile plinth, Capilla de las Doncellas (first half of the sixteenth century)

On the wall facing the *reja* is a canvas dating from the latter half of the eighteenth century, recalling dowries donated in the past. The Immaculate Conception in the glass case at the entrance to the chapel is a nineteenth-century work from the studio of Cristóbal Ramos. Lecterns dating from different periods are displayed in a Baroque case. Another smaller showcase contains a collection of reliquaries. The stained-glass window, showing Mary Magdalene washing Christ's feet, is by Arnao de Flandes and dates from 1554.

The North Transept

The vast canvas that hangs high up on the wall of the north transept – *The Proclamation of the Doctrine of the Immaculate Conception* (1953) – was specially painted for the cathedral by Alfonso Grosso and is one of the most recent acquisitions. Directly above is Arnao de Flandes's stained-glass window of the Assumption, completed in 1541. Arnao de Flandes was responsible for the other windows in the north transept, with the exception of that depicting the Resurrection (1558), which is by Carlos de Brujas.

54

Altar de la Asunción

The Altar de la Asunción (Altar of the Assumption), fronted by a *reja*, contains an early eighteenth-century altarpiece with a painting of the Assumption of the Virgin by the Italian school. It appears to be a replica of the one in the church of San Francisco el Grande in Madrid, believed to have been painted by the Genoese artist Gregorio Ferrari in the late seventeenth century. The altarpiece features reliefs that depict scenes from the life of the Virgin and images of St Charles Borromeo and St Philip Neri.

Altar de Nuestra Señora de Belén

The altarpiece for the Altar de Nuestra Señora de Belén (Altar of Our Lady of Bethlehem) was built in 1692 by Jerónimo Franco and houses Alonso Cano's famous painting of Our Lady of Bethlehem, dating from about 1635. The Holy Trinity, which crowns the entire altar, is the work of the Sevillian artist Virgilio Mattoni, completed in 1901. On the altar itself are two small statues of St Joachim and St Anne by Cristóbal Ramos. The Pietà, with the Eternal Father, was only recently placed on the left-hand wall; it is by Juan de Sevilla, a native of Granada, and is thought to have been painted in about 1670.

All the stained-glass windows in the remaining chapels leading off the north transept are by Enrique Alemán and date from 1478.

Capilla de San Francisco

The Capilla de San Francisco (Chapel of St Francis) is lit by a stained-glass window (1554-56) by Arnao de Flandes, which shows the Vision of St Francis. The altarpiece (1661), by Bernardo Simón de Pineda with gilding by Juan Gómez, has as its focal point a powerful, exquisitely composed and technically brilliant painting of the Ecstasy of St Francis (1656) by Francisco de Herrera the Younger. The painting of the Imposition of the Chasuble upon St Ildefonso (1661) by Juan de Valdés Leal is particularly striking for the naturalism of the saint's face.

Opposite the altarpiece is another, smaller painting, depicting St Teresa and thought to date from the first quarter of the seventeenth century. According to some authorities, the imagery of this altarpiece suggests that it may be the work of Pedro de Noguera, commissioned by the Monesión Convent in Seville and transferred to the cathedral in 1918. Another sculpture preserved in this chapel is a late seventeenth-century bust of an Ecce Homo.

The Conversion of St Paul, perhaps the chapel's most important canvas, is thought to be by the seventeenth-century Flemish artist Frans Francken II. The portrait of the Venerable Contreras was painted in Rome by José Preciado de la Vega in 1770. Hanging on the same wall is Ramón Bayeu's *St Sebastian*, painted in about the same year. *The Virgin of the People* (1508) is a copy of a painting in the Basilica of Santa Maria Maggiore in Rome. *Salome with the Head of John the Baptist*, dating from the mid-seventeenth century, is attributed to the Genoese painter Valerio Castello.

Music stands, delivered to the cathedral in 1723 and large enough to support the huge choir books used during Corpus Christi festivities, are now kept in the chapel. They are made of gilt and painted wood and are adorned with a variety of

Opposite: Francisco de Herrera
the Younger, *Ecstasy* (1657),
Capilla de San Francisco

Right: Juan de Valdés Leal,
*The Imposition of the Chasuble upon
St Ildefonsus* (1661), Capilla
de San Francisco

Below, right: Corpus Christi
music stand (1723), Capilla
de San Francisco

decorations, from plant motifs to cherubs with sheets of music. Other interesting pieces of furniture on display here are eighteenth-century litters and a late eighteenth-century lectern in the Rococo style.

Capilla de Santiago

The stained-glass window of the Capilla de Santiago (Chapel of St James the Apostle), showing the Conversion of St Paul, is by Vicente Menardo and dates from 1560. The altarpiece, by Bernardo Simón de Pineda and built in 1663, was designed to provide a framework for Juan de Roelas's powerful depiction of St James at the Battle of Clavijo, painted in 1609. At the top of the altarpiece is Valdés Leal's Martyrdom of St Laurence. The saint appears in the foreground as the centre of the composition, while his actual martyrdom can be seen in the background. The painting must have been commissioned at the same time as the altarpiece. On the altar table is an urn decorated with a polychrome wood Pietà, whose Baroque style suggests that it is an eighteenth-century Spanish work.

Another interesting feature of the chapel is the Gothic tomb of Archbishop Gonzálo de Mena, founder of the Carthusian Order in Seville. His effigy is in alabaster, and the sides of the tomb are decorated with scenes from the lives of Christ and the Virgin Mary. The tomb stands against a wall constructed in the fifteenth century, with a relief of the Madonna and Child in glazed terracotta, enamelled in white and blue. The relief, which came from the former Trinity Convent and is traditionally known as the Virgin of the Cushion, is believed to be from the studio of the Florentine sculptor Andrea della Robbia. On the same wall are the portraits of Sister Dorothea by Murillo and the Venerable Contreras by Luis de Vargas. Above them are small paintings of the Ecce Homo and Our Lady of Sorrows, attributed to followers of Murillo. The Creation cycle by the Dutch artist Simón de Vos, painted in 1644, shows the creation of the world, the creation of the birds and beasts, the division of light from darkness, the division of the waters and the land, the creation of Adam, and Cain slaying Abel.

A series of panels, which were once part of the former reliquary altarpiece in the Sacristía Mayor, appear on the wall opposite the altarpiece. They show allegorical scenes of those virtues that lead to the salvation of the soul. They were painted in about 1547 by the Sevillian artist Antón Pérez.

Capilla de Scalas

The Capilla de Scalas (Chapel of Scalas) is fronted by a magnificent Renaissance *reja* dating from 1564. The tympanum shows the Virgin and the Twelve Apostles in a formation reminiscent of the Tree of Jesse, each framed in a circlet of branches embossed in metal plate. The stained-glass window, which represents the Coming of the Holy Spirit, was made by F.X. Zettler in Munich and was installed in 1880. The two figures at prayer are the donors, the Precentor Cayetano Fernández and the Archpriest Jerónimo Álvarez Troya.

Although the chapel was originally dedicated to Our Lady of Consolation, it became known as the Capilla de Scalas after its founder, Baltasar del Río, Bishop of Scalas. He was in the service of popes Julius II and Leo X, who appointed him

Opposite: Workshop of the
Gazzini de Bissone family, Tomb
of Baltasar del Río (ca. 1539),
Capilla de Scalas

Opposite, below: Studio of
Andrea della Robbia, Virgen de
la Granada (fifteenth century),
Capilla de Scalas

Archdeacon of Niebla and Canon of Seville Cathedral. He financed the chapel from his stipend, which enabled him to maintain his own personal steward, organist, inspector and sexton. He also had the use of other rooms above the Patio de los Naranjos (these were demolished at the beginning of the twentieth century).

In 1521, the Bishop of Scalas decided to have a tomb built for himself in the chapel at the foot of the altar. The tomb with the recumbent figure of the bishop is in the lower part of the chapel. The recess in which it lies is decorated with a circular relief of the Madonna and Child and statues of St Peter and St Paul. However, the bishop was never buried there. He died in Rome in 1541 and was laid to rest in that city's church of Santiago de los Españoles (Spanish Church of St James).

Standing on a low tribune immediately above the sacristy is a magnificent marble altarpiece, installed on 5 May 1539. The high degree of craftsmanship and exquisite composition suggest that it was made in the workshop of the Italian Gazzini de Bissone family. It is framed by Corinthian columns supporting an entablature; this in turn provides the base for a pediment containing a relief of the Eternal Father. In the centre is a large relief depicting the Pentecost. On the predella is a relief of the Miracle of the Loaves and the Fishes, flanked by a portrait of the Bishop of Scalas at prayer and his coat-of-arms.

Another of the chapel's magnificent works of art is the enamelled terracotta Virgen de la Granada (Virgin of the Pomegranate), so called because the Madonna is offering a pomegranate to the Christ Child seated on her lap. Two angels hold a crown above her head while St Francis and St Dominic stand beside her on her right and St Casilda and St Sebastian on her left. Above the Virgen is a series of cherubim and then a semicircular arch, which contains a relief of Christ, Man of Sorrows, flanked by St John and the Virgin Mary. The relief, which was for many years in the Patio de los Naranjos, is thought to have been made in the workshop of Andrea della Robbia in Florence.

Among the paintings in the chapel is an interesting Holy Family, reminiscent of Murillo, executed by Juan Ruiz Soriano in about 1740. The St Ferdinand is also the work of one of Murillo's disciples and is believed to have been painted around 1675. The Pietà, dating from 1666, is by the Sevillian artist Sebastián de Llanos Valdés. There is also a mid-sixteenth-century panel showing the Kiss of Judas and an Ecce Homo. A collection of reliquaries and a Gothic marble Madonna and Child are displayed in a small showcase.

Capilla de San Antonio or del Bautismo

The Capilla de San Antonio (Chapel of St Anthony), also known as the Capilla del Bautismo (Baptistry Chapel), is lit by a stained-glass window by Juan Bautista de Léon dating from 1685. It shows St Justa and St Rufina, and the Vision of St Anthony. In 1813, so as to admit more light, the original blue background was substituted for the present white one. Standing in the centre of the chapel is a large sixteenth-century marble baptismal font; the base is decorated in the Renaissance style with figures of dancing angels.

The altarpiece, a painting of the Vision of St Anthony, is not only one of the cathedral's most famous works of art, but also among the best known of Bartolomé Esteban Murillo's paintings. It is a work on the grand scale; its diagonal

composition creates immense tension between the kneeling saint on the right of the picture and the Christ Child, who floats weightlessly in a blaze of glory. On 4 November 1874 the painting was badly damaged by an art thief who cut out the figure of St Anthony and tried to sell it to an antique dealer in New York. Recognizing the provenance of the figure, the dealer bought it and returned it to the city's Spanish Consulate. Shortly afterwards, the painting was restored by Salvador Martínez Cubells and reinstalled in its rightful place in the chapel. A wide moulding, crafted by Bernardo Simón de Pineda in 1668, runs from *The Vision of St Antony* to *The Baptism of Christ*, another of Murillo's finest works, which has been executed with dazzling fluency and technical mastery.

Two major works of art have recently been placed on the wall adjoining the altarpiece. The first, *The Virgin of the Elm Trees*, stood for many years overlooking the courtyard of the same name behind the apse of the cathedral and was subsequently moved to the lower part of the Giralda. The second is a beam with nineteen paintings thought to date from the first quarter of the sixteenth century. The panels in the centre depict the Pietà while those to the sides show Apostles and Prophets. Next to these are representations of St Leander and St Isidore, and St Justa and St Rufina, highly reminiscent of the style of Ignacio de Ríes and dating from around 1660. The portrait of the Blessed Juan de Ribera is by an anonymous nineteenth-century painter. On the opposite wall is a series of paintings of varying artistic merit. The Immaculate Conception is attributed to the seventeenth-century

Capilla de San Antonio

Above, left: Bartolomé Esteban Murillo, *The Vision of St Antony* (1654)

Above: Bartolomé Esteban Murillo, *The Baptism of Christ* (1668)

Opposite: Painted beam, detail

Sevillian painter Francisco Varela. The Madonna and Child is a later work, thought to have been painted by a follower of Murillo. St Peter praying before Christ bound to a pillar is from the same period. The most interesting work in this collection is *The Imposition of the Palium on St Isidore*, attributed to Lucas Valdés.

Portada del Sagrario

After the baptismal font that originally stood here was removed to the Capilla de San Antonio, the Portada del Sagrario (Portal of the Sacrament) was installed to link the cathedral to the new Iglesia del Sagrario (Church of the Sacrament) on the west side of the Patio de los Naranjos. Work on the Church of El Sagrario began in 1618, to plans by the architects Miguel de Zumárraga, Alonso de Vandelvira and Cristóbal de Rojas. The double colonnade along the west side of the ablutions courtyard of the former mosque was removed to make way for the new church.

The portal was designed by Pedro Sánchez Falconete in 1655. It consists of a triangular pediment flanked by Corinthian columns topped by niches. The frieze and spandrels of the lower part are decorated with plant motifs, while the tympanum is adorned with scrolls. The sculptures of St Ferdinand, St Isidore, St Leander, St Justa and St Rufina are particularly fine.

Flanking the portal are reliefs (1581-84) carved by Diego de Velasco and Juan Bautista Vázquez the Elder. They represent the Fathers of the Church and the Evangelists and originally adorned the old chests of drawers in the Main Sacristy.

A showcase containing a selection of books from the choir library now stands in front of the portal. The library was established in the first quarter of the fifteenth century and still boasts a fascinating collection of some 300 volumes. Among the best known contemporary illuminators was El Maestro de los Cipreses (Master of the Cypresses), whose real name appears to have been Pedro de Toledo. Books of the period are decorated with filigree designs, although the most interesting miniatures occur on the edges and in the decorations of capital letters. Among the most important items in the collection are the sixteenth-century choir books bearing such names as Rodrigo de León, Pedro Vizcaíno, Diego de Orta and Jerónimo de Orta. The tradition of illuminated books survived into the seventeenth and eighteenth centuries, and there are some notable examples from this period in the choir library.

Left: El Maestro de los Cipreses, *The Nativity* (first half of the fifteenth century)

Opposite: Diego de Orta, Santa María Magdalena (1567)

Western Chapels

Capilla de los Jácomes

The Capilla de los Jácomes (Chapel of the Jácomes), also known as the Capilla de las Angustias (Chapel of Sorrows), was originally founded by a community of Flemish knights in Seville. In the seventeenth century it passed into the hands of the Marquesses of Tablantes, whose surname was Jácomes. The Baroque plasterwork on the walls and ceiling dates from around 1675. The altarpiece was made in 1658 by the Cordoban artist Francisco Dionisio de Ribas and is crowned with the Holy Countenance and figures of Faith and Hope. The Pietà (1609) by Juan de Roelas is unfortunately in poor condition. On the side wall is a panel of the Assumption of the Virgin attributed to the Flemish painter Marcel Coffermans.

Altar de la Visitación

The Altar de la Visitación (Altar of the Visitation) is fronted by a *reja* dating from 1568. The altarpiece, dating from 1566 and commissioned by the cathedral Chaplain

Jerónimo Hernández,
St Jerome Penitent (1566),
Altar de la Visitación

Matías de Figueroa and Diego
Castillejo, façade of the Capilla
de San Leandro (1733-4)

Diego de Bolaños, comprises a relief of St Jerome Penitent by Jerónimo Hernández
and paintings by Pedro de Villegas Marmolejo. The central painting, a scene of the
Visitation on which are inscribed the words '*Petrus Villegas Pintor Faciebat*' ('Pedro de
Villegas painter made this'), shows the extent to which Villegas was influenced by
artists such as Campaña, Esturmio and Vargas. St Blaise, the Baptism of Christ, St
James and St Sebastian appear on the side panels of the altarpiece. The donor and
members of his family are portrayed on the predella.

    Above the Puerta del Bautismo, between the Altar de la Visitación and the
Capilla de San Leandro, is a stained-glass window of the Visitation (1566) by
Vicente Menardo.

Capilla de San Leandro

The entrance to the Capilla de San Leandro (Chapel of St Leander) consists of a
lavish portal, designed by Matías de Figueroa and Diego Castillejo between 1733
and 1734. A pair of altars, with niches, flank the *reja*; this, a copy of the *reja* in the
Capilla de San Isidoro, was made by Francisco de Guzmán and Francisco de
Ocampo the Younger, and it dates from the about the same period as the portal.

    The two stained-glass windows date from 1770. The Baroque altarpiece, by
Manuel de Escobar, dates from 1730. In the centre is a statue of St Leander by the
Cordoban sculptor Pedro Duque Cornejo, who was also responsible for St
Fulgentius and St Anthony Abbot on either side and St Dominic Guzman on the

crest. The paintings of St Leander instructing St Florentina and of St Leander at the Council of Toledo are by J. Mausola and date from 1735.

Altar de Nuestra Señora de la Alcobilla

The small altarpiece in the Altar de Nuestra Señora de la Alcobilla (Altar of Our Lady of the Little Alcove) dates from 1735 and houses a polychrome terracotta sculpture of the Pietà, thought to be of Flemish provenance and dating from around 1500. It is popularly known as Our Lady of the Little Alcove.

Altar del Niño Mudo

The Altar del Niño Mudo (Altar of the Dumb Christ Child), dating from about 1735, takes its name from the statue of the Infant Jesus on the altar that is popularly known as the Dumb Child. For many years it was incorrectly attributed to Juan Martínez Montañés. It is in fact a copy, made in the second half of the seventeenth century, of an original by Montañés belonging to the Holy Brotherhood of the Sagrario, and is inferior to the work of this master. The altar frontal was designed by José Gestoso and made by Manuel Rodríguez Pérez de Tudela in 1909.

Altar del Consuelo

The Altar del Consuelo (Altar of the Consolation), a small chapel framed by a Gothic portal, has as its altarpiece a painting of the Virgin of Consolation (1720) by Alonso Miguel de Tovar. The Virgin is shown holding the Infant Jesus on her lap with St Anthony of Padua and St James the Apostle on either side. At her feet is Don Diego López de Enciso, who financed the construction of the altar and who is buried at its foot. Certain marks visible beneath Tovar's painting reveal that the work was painted on a Gothic panel.

Altar del Ángel de la Guarda

The Altar del Ángel de la Guarda (Altar of the Guardian Angel), which is very similar to the Altar del Consuelo, houses one of Murillo's most famous canvases, *The Guardian Angel*. It was painted in 1665 for the Capuchin Convent in Seville, which later donated it to the cathedral chapter.

Capilla de San Isidoro

The portal to the Capilla de San Isidoro (Chapel of St Isidore) was built in 1661 under the patronage of the Puente Verástegui family. The exuberantly decorative scheme incorporates a pair of small altars dedicated respectively to the Virgin of the Strawberries and the Virgin of the Girdle. It was the model for the portal of the Capilla de San Leandro, whose craftsmen also copied a number of other features in the chapels at the west end of the cathedral. The chapel's *reja* provided the model for that in the Capilla de San Leandro. The interior of the chapel is decorated with Baroque plasterwork with shields and scrolls that were originally painted in

polychrome. The altarpiece on the main wall, dated 1664, was carved by Bernardo Simón de Pineda and gilded by Agustín Franco and Juan de Valdés Leal. Pineda also carved the sacristy door. The sculptures on the altarpiece represent St Isidore, St Leander, St Francis and St James of Alcalá.

Altar de la Virgen del Madroño

The Altar de la Virgen del Madroño (Altar of the Virgin of the Strawberries) takes its name from its altarpiece, an alabaster group of the Virgin of the Strawberries (c. 1455), attributed to Lorenzo Mercadante de Bretaña. The statue shows the Virgin offering her breast to the Christ Child, who looks out towards the spectator, as if giving His blessing. An angel kneels before them offering a basket of strawberries.

Altar de la Virgen de la Cinta

In the Altar de la Virgen de la Cinta (Altar of the Virgin of the Girdle), a statue of the Virgin with the Christ Child in her arms stands within a simple gilt altarpiece dating from the seventeenth century. The statue, a work of great beauty, is attributed to Lorenzo Mercadante de Bretaña (the girdle that hangs from the Virgin's waist giving the chapel its name) and shares similarities with other works executed by the artist in the 1460s.

Above: Lorenzo Mercadante de Bretaña, *The Virgin of the Strawberries* (ca. 1455), Capilla de la Virgen del Madroño

Right: Luis de Vargas, *The Adoration of the Shepherds* (1555), Altar del Nacimiento

Altar del Nacimiento

The Altar del Nacimiento (Altar of the Nativity) is dominated by a painted altarpiece by the Sevillian artist Luis de Vargas, who completed the work in 1555. The central painting of the Adoration of the Shepherds reflects the extent to which Vargas was influenced by the followers of Raphael as the result of his visit to Italy. The other paintings of which the altarpiece consists depict the Annunciation, the Presentation of Jesus in the Temple, St John, St Luke, St Matthew, St Mark and the Adoration of the Magi. Both the altarpiece and the *reja*, which date from the sixteenth century, were donated by the merchant Francisco de Baena.

Above the Nativity Door is a stained-glass window (1566) by Vicente Menardo, which represents the Annunciation.

Southern Chapels

The stained-glass windows above the first four chapels off the cathedral's south aisle are by Enrique Alemán and were made between 1478 and 1479.

Capilla de San Laureano

The Capilla de San Laureano (Chapel of St Laureano), dedicated to one of Seville's earliest archbishops, was the burial chapel of Alonso de Egea, Patriarch of Constantinople and Archbishop of Seville, who died in 1417. The *reja* dates from 1702 and the chapel is lit by a stained-glass window, completed by Vicente Menardo in 1572, showing St Isidore, St Laureano and St Leander.

At the beginning of the eighteenth century, Valentín Lampérez y Blázquez, canon of the cathedral, made arrangements for his burial in the chapel and ordered changes to the decoration. His tombstone is still preserved. The altarpiece was built in about 1700. In the centre of lower section, between barley-sugar columns, stands a statue of St Laureano in archbishop's vestments and with a dagger in his hand. Reliefs to left and right respectively show St Laureano at prayer and the Angel appearing to him. In the centre of the upper section is a relief showing the martyrdom of St Laureano. When the chapel was remodelled, the vaults and walls were decorated with murals by Lucas Valdés; these have now almost all disappeared.

At about the same time, Matías de Arteaga was commissioned to produce a cycle of paintings of scenes from the life of St Laureano. They include *The Raising from the Dead of a Young Man in Marseilles*, *St Laureano before Pope Virgil*, *St Laureano Healing a Cripple*, *The Martyrdom of St Laureano*, and *The Head of St Laureano Delivered to the Clergy of Seville*. This latter painting is particularly interesting, since it features a view of Seville with the city's Puerta del Arenal, the cathedral and the Giralda in the background.

Opposite the altarpiece is the tomb of Cardinal Joaquín Lluch y Garriga, who died in 1882. Its statue of the cardinal kneeling at prayer, on a plinth guarded at each corner by angels, was completed three years later by the Catalan sculptor Agapito Valmitjana.

Capilla de Santa Ana or del Cristo de Maracaibo

The Capilla de Santa Ana (Chapel of St Anne), also known as the Capilla del Cristo de Maracaibo (Chapel of the Holy Christ of Maracaibo), has been dedicated to several saints since it was built. The first was St Bartholomew, to whom the altarpiece is dedicated. It was later dedicated to St Anne, and until recently the painting of St Anne with the Madonna and Child, a copy after Giambattista Carraciolo (now on display in the Sacristía de los Calices), hung there. The chapel was finally rededicated to the Holy Christ of Maracaibo after the eponymous painting of the Crucifixion that was placed there in the eighteenth century.

The two inscription panels at the base of the altarpiece read:

Left panel:
ESTE RE
TABLO
MANDO FA
ÇER EL RE
VERENDO
S. DIEGO
HER[N]ADEZ
MAR[T]OLE
ARÇEDIANO
DE L OIJA
CAN[O]NICO
DELA Sta
[I]GLE SIA

Right panel:
E EL
[H]ONRADO
CAVALERO
RVI
BARBA
[S]V ...VJ[O]
AGAB[O]SE
E EL MES ...
E TE[N]...
... O D ...
... O.A

The chapel, separated from the aisle by a simple *reja*, is lit by a stained-glass window (1797) of the Holy Family. The altarpiece stands on a tribune, beneath which there is access to the cathedral's administrative offices. Two different artists, commissioned by Canon Diego Hernández de Marmolejo, built the altarpiece, which was completed in 1504. The scenes depicted on the predella are the Flagellation, the Road to Calvary, the Crucifixion, the Descent from the Cross and the Pietà. The lower section shows St Bartholomew with St James and St Blaise on his left and St Nicholas and St Sebastian on his right. In the upper section is a Gothic statue of the Madonna and Child with St John the Baptist and St Anne on her left and St Martha and St Michael on her right. The style of the Madonna and Child shows distinctively Flemish and French influences.

Opposite the entrance is a modern altarpiece by Joaquín Bilbao, commissioned by the Count and Countess of Galindo to house a very interesting painting thought to date from the 1560s. Some authorities claim that the panel shares many similarities with the works of Pedro Villegas Marmolejo. Joaquín Bilbao also carved the reliefs of the Madonna and St John.

Against the wall opposite the altarpiece is the tomb of Cardinal Luis de Lastra y Cuesta, built in 1880 by Ricardo Bellver. The cardinal is shown kneeling at prayer on a marble plinth with angels seated at each corner.

Other noteworthy paintings in the chapel include an Immaculate Conception by a follower of Murillo; *Abraham and the Three Angels*, attributed to the seventeenth-century Flemish artist Abraham Van Diepenbeek; and *Christ Served by the Angels*, a work thought to have links with Juan de Uceda. Also noteworthy are the copper reliefs of the Marriage at Cana and the Miracle of the Loaves and Fishes, dating from the second half of the seventeenth century. There is also an appealing painting by Lucas Valdés of the silver throne shown as it was used in Corpus Christi ceremonies during the eighteenth century.

Capilla de San José

The Capilla de San José (Chapel of St Joseph), lit by a modern stained-glass window, dates from 1932. The centrepiece of the chapel is a late eighteenth-century Neo-classical marble altarpiece by Pedro de Arnal. The statue of St Joseph was sculpted by Jose Esteve, while those of St Michael and St Blaise, as well as the statues at the top of the altarpiece, are by Alfonso Bergaz.

The tomb of Cardinal Joaquín Tarancón, built in about 1865, stands opposite the altarpiece. The most interesting paintings in the chapel are of the Sacrifice of Isaac (1660) by Llanos Valdés, and the Twelve Apostles (c. 1700), possibly by Estebán Márquez. Also kept in the chapel is the image of the Flagellation, which originally formed part of the Maundy Thursday monument by Francisco Antonio Gijón.

The tomb of Cardinal José María Bueno y Monreal was recently installed against the wall facing the *reja*.

Capilla de San Hermenegildo

In the centre of the Capilla de San Hermenegildo (Chapel of St Hermenegild) stands the tomb of Cardinal Juan Cervantes. The sepulchre is decorated on all four sides with angels supporting the cardinal's coat-of-arms; this is reminiscent of the drawings of the Flemish painter Jan van Eyck, and upon it lies the recumbent figure of the cardinal. The face, based on the cardinal's death mask, is remarkably realistic. The tomb (1453-58) bears the inscription '*Lorenzo Mercadante de Bretaña entalló este bulto*' ('Lorenzo Mercadante de Bretaña carved this piece').

The chapel's altarpiece was built in the mid-eighteenth century by the sculptor Manuel García de Santiago. It consists of a predella, central section and pediment, vertically divided by tapering pillars. The statue of the Sevillian martyr St Hermenegild, which forms the centrepiece, is the work of Bartolomé García Santiago, father of Manuel. On the altar are two outstanding sculptures; one is of St James the Less, shown carrying the cudgel symbolizing the manner in which he met his death. It is believed to be one of the images in the cathedral dome to have survived when the dome collapsed in 1511. Carved in stone, it was later repainted, but the exquisite craftsmanship and the beautifully detailed pleats of the saint's robe are still clearly visible. The other statue, of St James the Apostle, by an anonymous mid-fifteenth-century artist, is in painted wood.

At the foot of the chapel is the tomb of Juan Mate de Luna, Lord High Admiral of Castile, who died in 1337 and whose remains were moved to the chapel from the Puerta del Lagarto in 1848.

Among the paintings in the chapel the most outstanding are three seventeenth-century works by the Flemish artist Frans Francken: *The Marriage at Cana*, *Salome with the Head of John the Baptist*, and *Belshazzar's Feast*. Of lesser artistic merit are *St Engracia* and *St Rufina*, attributed to folllowers of Zurbarán, and *Christ and the Woman taken in Adultery*, a seventeenth-century work in the Italian style. The *Virgen de la Antigua* is an eighteenth-century copy, and St Librada, dating from the same period, is interesting for its pictorial content.

The simple stained-glass window, portraying St Hermenegild, dates from 1819.

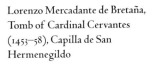

Lorenzo Mercadante de Bretaña, Tomb of Cardinal Cervantes (1453–58), Capilla de San Hermenegildo

Left: Capilla de la Virgen de la Antigua

Opposite: La Antigua (late fourteenth century), Capilla de la Virgen de la Antigua

Capilla de la Virgen de la Antigua

The Capilla de la Virgen de la Antigua was originally dedicated to a painting of the Madonna that once stood in the old mosque-cathedral and is thus known as La Antigua (The Ancient One). The chapel was originally exactly the same size and shape as the others. However, at the end of the fifteenth century, when Cardinal Diego Hurtado de Mendoza chose it as his burial chapel, it was enlarged, its height was doubled and a sacristy was added. The architect was Simón de Colonia, who was also involved with the design of the complex rib-vaulted ceiling. In 1734, another architect, Diego Antonio Díaz, began repairs to the ceiling as part of the renovation of the chapel, commissioned by Archbishop Luis de Salcedo y Azcona, whose burial chapel it was also to be.

The portal leading into the chapel from the south transept may have been designed by Diego de Riaño but it was not built until about 1535, probably by Martín de Gainza. Above it is a relief of the Nativity and the figure of God the Father, with Apostles occupying the inner surface of the arch and columns' capitals. The *reja* was designed by Miguel de Zumárraga and constructed by Hernando de Pineda.

The process of creating the chapel's main *reja*, one of the most monumental in the cathedral, was long and complex. Although records refer to various plans drawn up during the first half of the sixteenth century, work on the *reja* did not start until 1565, when Juan López was appointed to carry out the work, to a design by Hernán Ruiz the Younger. In 1572 another craftsman, Juan Barba, took over. After a few years, the architect Asensio de Maeda was asked to make certain modifications. Juan Barba continued working on the *reja* but never completed it. Rodrigo de Segovia completed the project at the beginning of the seventeenth century, and the gilding and polychrome were applied later.

The interior of the chapel is lit by a late nineteenth-century stained-glass window showing Ferdinand III enthroned. It was designed by José Gestoso and

made by F. X. Zettler. The altarpiece, of coloured marble and jasper, was
commissioned by Archbishop Luis de Salcedo y Azcona to house the Virgen de la
Antigua. It was designed by Duque Cornejo (who was also responsible for the
sculptures) and built by Juan Fernández de Iglesias. In the lower section, St Joachim
and St Anne appear on either side of the Madonna. Above them the figure of Christ
is flanked by St John the Baptist and St John the Evangelist.

The Virgen de la Antigua is a late fourteenth-century fresco that has undergone
a number of alterations since it was originally painted. In 1578 the pillar close to
the present main *reja*, on which the image was painted, was moved to its present
position. The Virgin is depicted with a rose in her hand, while the Christ Child
holds a bird. Two angels hold a silver crown, made in 1929 by Granda Builla, above
the Virgin's head. The unusually small kneeling figure is the benefactrice, Doña
Leonor de Alburquerque.

The chapel also contains fine silverwork. The Rococo altar frontal, dating from
the late eighteenth century, shows the Virgin appearing to St Ferdinand. The second
altar has a silver frontal from the same period. The altar rail is also of silver, as are
the sixty or so hanging lamps, completed in 1738. The chandelier in the centre of the
chapel was donated by the silver merchant Juan de Ochoa in 1672.

At the same time that the painting of the Virgin was moved, the two doorways in
the chapel presbytery were built, almost certainly to a design by Asensio de Maeda.
Renovations, which began in 1734, include the addition of the tortoiseshell, ebony
and bronze doors, adorned with the coat-of-arms of the donor, Archbishop
Salcedo y Azcona.

Two interesting tombs stand against the chapel's side walls. The one on the left is
that of Cardinal Diego Hurtado de Mendoza. It was built in Genoa by Domenico
Fancelli, who came to Seville in 1510 to install it in its present place. The tomb
stands on a plinth within an arch. Surrounding the recumbent figure of the
cardinal are decorative motifs, such as statues of saints, reliefs depicting scenes
from the Gospels and the coats-of-arms of the deceased. Opposite is the tomb
of Archbishop Luis Salcedo y Azcona, built in 1734 by Pedro Duque Cornejo to
harmonize with the cardinal's tomb and maintain the balance of the chapel.

The cycle of paintings on the walls, recounting the history of the Virgen de la
Antigua, was executed by Domingo Martínez and Andrés Rubira between 1734 and
1738. On the upper part of the right-hand wall, the Virgin is shown appearing to the
Moors; the central section shows the removal of the image of the Virgin, with St
Leander and St Laureano on either side. In the lower part the Venerable Contreras
presents prisoners to the Virgin, with four oval portraits of St Louis of France, St
Louis of Toulouse, St Louis Gonzaga and St Louis Beltrán. Beside the altar is a
portrait of Sister María de Agreda.

On the upper part of the left-hand wall is a depiction of the mosque wall
collapsing to reveal the image of the Virgin. The focal point of the central section is
St Ferdinand's nocturnal visit to the Virgin, with St Carpoforus and St Isidore on
either side. Below are St James of Alcalá healing the sick, Christ restoring the sight
of a blind man, and four oval portraits of St Ferdinand, St Florentina (sister of St
Isidore), St Hermenegild and St Abundio. Beside the altar is a portrait of the
medieval Scottish philosopher John Duns Scotus. Some paintings were destroyed in
a fire in 1889 and were replaced by others on similar themes but of lesser quality.

South Transept

Altar de la Concepción

The *reja* of the Altar de la Concepción (Altar of the Immaculate Conception) was begun by Juan Méndez and completed in 1562 by Pedro Delgado, working to a design by Hernán Ruiz the Younger, which modified the earlier plan.

The altarpiece, donated by Don Juan de Medina, is a brilliant example of the work of the Sevillian artist Luis de Vargas. It was built in 1561 and takes the form of an allegory of the Immaculate Conception inspired by a painting by the Italian artist and biographer Giorgio Vasari. The figures are disposed around the Tree of Jesse, showing the line of descent from Adam to the Virgin Mary. The paintings on the predella consist of an allegory of the Church and a portrait of Precentor Medina with his coat-of-arms. In the sides are paintings of St Peter and St Paul.

Monument to Christopher Columbus

The monument to Christopher Columbus, discoverer of America, stands in the centre of the south transept. In 1891, the chapter of Havana Cathedral commissioned Antonio Mélida to design a tomb to hold Columbus's remains. In 1898, as the result of Cuban independence, the monument was shipped to Seville, and it has stood in Seville Cathedral ever since. It consists of four heralds, symbolizing the four kingdoms of the Spanish Crown, bearing the coffin of the great navigator on their shoulders.

The wall to the left of the monument is filled with vast fresco of St Christopher painted by the Italian artist Mateo Pérez de Alesio in 1584. The palette and composition of the painting show the influence of the Roman Mannerist style of the Zuccaro family. On the tribune above the entrance to the Altar of La Piedad is the austere Neo-classical clock made by Brother José Cordero in 1789. Above it is Arnao de Vergara's stained-glass window of the Assumption, dating from 1536.

The other windows in the south transept are by Arnao de Flandes, except that of St Hermenegild, St Jerome and St Eustace, which date from 1929. The windows above the remaining chapels off the south side were made by Arnao de Flandes between 1555 and 1556.

Altar de la Piedad

The Altar de la Piedad (Altar of Mercy) is fronted by a sixteenth-century *reja*. The altarpiece, donated by Doña Mencia de Salazar, is by Alejo Fernández and dates from 1527. The main panel is devoted to the Pietà, with St John and St Joseph of Arimathea, and the three Marys. The predella shows St Peter and Christ bound to a pillar, flanked by portraits of Doña Mencia and her husband Don Alonso Pérez

de Medina. To each side are paintings of St Andrew, St Michael, St James and St Francis.

Capilla de los Dolores

The *reja* of the Capilla de los Dolores (Chapel of Sorrows), commissioned from José Guío by the cathedral chapter in 1787, is of interest in that it replaces the cathedral's last surviving wooden screen. It incorporates a small stained-glass window, dated 1931, which contains the coat-of-arms of Cardinal Ilundain.

The chapel's eighteenth-century altarpiece is divided by tapered pilasters. In the centre of the predella is a richly dressed figure of Our Lady of Sorrows dating from around 1680 and attributed to Pedro de Mena y Medrano, of Granada. The late sixteenth-century Crucifix in the central niche above is attributed to a follower of Bautista Vázquez the Elder. To either side are paintings from the eighteenth century, depicting the Virgin, St John, two angels and the Eternal Father.

Occupying the left wall of the chapel is the tomb of Cardinal Marcelo Spinola y Maestre. It was built by Joaquín Bilbao y Martínez and completed in 1912. The figure of the cardinal kneels in prayer before a relief of the Immaculate Conception.

Several interesting paintings hang on the left wall. The most important is *Jacob Blessing his Sons*, attributed to the seventeenth-century Flemish artist Pieter Van Lint. *Peter Denying Christ*, which displays the influence of Caravaggio, is probably by a French follower of Bartholomeo Manfredi. *The Entombment* is by an anonymous French follower of Trophime Bigot, which dates from around 1620. The painting of

the Madonna and Child, by a follower of Pedro Millán, on the wall adjoining the altar, has recently been transferred here from the Puerta del Lagarto.

The most remarkable object in the chapel is the magnificent *tenebrario*, a bronze and wooden candelabrum designed for use in services held during Holy Week. (Because of changes in the liturgy, it is no longer used.) The *tenebrario*, described by Ceán Bermudez, the nineteenth-century Spanish art historian as 'the finest piece of its kind in Spain', was designed by Hernán Ruiz II, the cathedral's greatest master craftsman, and made between 1559 and 1562. Faithfully following his design, the lower section of the candelabrum was modelled by the *rejero* Pedro Delgado and cast by Bartolomé Morel. The upper section was modelled by Juan de Giralte and Juan Bautista Vázquez the Elder and cast later. The pedestal incorporates a figure of Hermes, messenger of the gods. Various human figures appear in the medallion at the base of the main section. The statuettes that crown it represent the Twelve Apostles, while the Virgin appears in the central section. Since they have lost their special attributes, two of the statuettes are difficult to identify.

Sacristía de los Cálices

The Sacristía de los Cálices (Sacristy of the Chalices) is reached through the Capilla de los Dolores. Its rectangular floor plan is extended at the far end to accommodate two small chapels. The unevenness in the height of the ceiling is caused by the staircase in the adjacent Patio de los Óleos. The sacristy is divided into three different-sized sections by four Gothic pilasters linked by slender ribs. The rib vaulting is at different heights, and the main section rests on arches. The sloping lateral vaults fit into ducts where they adjoin the walls. The sacristy was designed by the architect Alonso Rodríguez, who began its construction. This was later continued by Juan Gil de Hontañón, Diego de Riaños and Martín de Gainza, who completed the ceiling in 1537.

Artefacts from the cathedral's collection are traditionally kept here. A collection of chalices dating from the seventeenth, eighteenth and nineteenth centuries is displayed in the two showcases on either side of the entrance to the sacristy. The most striking is the golden chalice, donated in 1744 by Juan Antonio Vizarrón, Archbishop of Mexico and former Archdeacon of Seville Cathedral. The two small chapels at the south end of the sacristy contain various pieces of seventeenth-century silverware, mostly salvers.

The paintings to the left of the entrance include some works of outstanding quality. Notable is the *Madonna with St Peter and St Jerome* attributed to the fifteenth-century artist Juan Sánchez de Castro, but with numerous restorations to the lower section. On the west wall are four large paintings originally intended for the beam of the high altar, painted by Alejo Fernández between 1508 and 1512. They are *St Joachim and St Anne Embracing*, *The Birth of the Virgin*, *The Adoration of the Magi*, and *The Presentation of Christ in the Temple*. Next to them is another large panel of St Peter, dating from 1528 and widely believed to be by Pedro Fernández de Guadalupe.

The south wall is dominated by *St Justa and St Rufina*, a large canvas by Francisco de Goya, painted in 1817 to a commission by the cathedral chapter. This is one of Goya's most beautiful religious paintings and depicts the two saints set serenely against a background of the River Guadalquivir, with the Giralda in the distance.

Opposite: Alejo Fernández,
The Adoration of the Magi (1508-12),
Sacristía de los Cálices

Above, left: Francisco de Goya,
St Justa and St Rufina (1817),
Sacristía de los Cálices

Above, right: Matía Preti,
The Guardian Ángel (ca.1660),
Sacristía de los Cálices

Right: Juan Nuñez, *Pietà*
(late fifteenth century),
Sacristía de los Cálices

Left: Francisco de Zurbarán,
St John the Baptist (ca. 1640),
Sacristía de los Cálices

Below: Juan de Valdés Leal,
*Lazarus with Martha and Mary
Magdalene* (ca. 1660), Sacristía
de los Cálices

Juan de Roelas, *Christ in Glory* (ca. 1615), Sacristía de los Cálices

On the east wall, starting from the right, is *St Jerome Penitent*, painted by Pablo Legot in about 1640, which reveals how the artist's acquaintance with the work of Jusepe de Ribera had a major influence on his own creativity. Nearby, on the upper part of the wall, is a depiction of the Circumcision (1669) by Jacob Jordaens. Next to it is the *Guardian Angel* by the Italian artist Matía Preti, dating from around 1660. The final painting in this upper section is the *Adoration of the Magi*, painted by Jordaens at about the same time. On the lower part of the wall is another painting from the same period, Valdés Leal's *Lazarus with Martha and Mary Magdalene*. Alongside are Juan Nuñez's late fifteenth-century Pietà, and a Christ in Glory, for many years attributed to Tintoretto but now known to be the work of Juan de Roelas, one of Seville's closest followers of the Venetian school. The last picture in this section is Zurbarán's *St John the Baptist*, dating from around 1640. Hanging on the next section of the wall is a Holy Trinity (1624) by Luis Tristán, clearly showing how strongly the artist was influenced by his teacher, El Greco. Next to this is a Crucifixion by Juan Sánchez de Román, painted in the final third of the fifteenth century. The final work on this wall is Valdés Leal's *Liberation of St Peter*, dating from around 1650.

The various works on the wall to the right of the entrance include, on the upper part, *St Anne with the Madonna and Child*, a copy of the original in Vienna by Giambattista Caracciolo. Beneath this is *St John the Baptist* by Zurbarán, painted around 1640. Above the entrance door is a Crucifixion, also by Zurbarán.

Capilla de San Andrés

The Capilla de San Andrés (Chapel of St Andrew) has a wrought-iron *reja* dating from the sixteenth century, with some later additions, such as the reliefs at either end. The chapel now contains one of the cathedral's most significant works of art and one of the finest examples of Andalusian polychrome sculpture, *Our Lord of Mercy*, also known as Christ of the Chalices, named after the Sacristía de los Cálices, where it was kept until recently. It was carved by Juan Martínez Montañés and painted by Francisco Pacheco. It was commissioned in 1603 by Mateo Vázques de Leca, Archdeacon of Carmona, for his private chapel, and was later donated to the Carthusian monastery of Santa María de las Cuevas in Seville, whence it was subsequently acquired by the cathedral. It is a serene work, with perfectly balanced, elongated lines. Christ is shown with His feet crossed and secured to the Cross by

Capilla de San Andrés

Below, left: Juan Martínez Montañés, *Our Lord of Mercy* (1603)

Opposite, above: Attributed to Ferrán González, Tombs of the Pérez de Guzmán y Ayala family (ca. 1400)

Opposite, below: Francesco Solimena, *The Transfer of the Ark of the Covenant* (ca. 1700)

four nails, as He was seen by St Bridget in her vision. The chapel also contains the tombs of the Pérez de Guzmán y Ayala family. These are not only among the most beautiful pieces of sculpture in the cathedral but also the oldest; they were previously housed in the old cathedral. They bear the effigies of Don Álvaro Pérez de Guzmán y Ayala the Elder, his wife Doña Elvira de Ayala and their son. On the opposite wall is the tomb of Don Alfonso Pérez de Guzmán. All four were originally in the centre of the chapel and were moved to their present position in 1796. They are believed to have been made in the studio of Ferrán González in Toledo between the end of fifteenth century and the early sixteenth.

Two large canvases, attributed to Francisco Solimena, a Neapolitan follower of Lucas Jordán, hang on the side walls. The painting on the left is the *Transfer of the Ark of the Covenant*, while that on the right represents the *Canticle of the Prophetess María*. Both are believed to date from the early eighteenth century.

Higher up the walls are two more paintings: that on the left is a Crucifixion, a copy after the Italian artist Scipione Pulzone, dated around 1590; that on the right is the *Martyrdom of St Andrew*, a late eighteenth-century copy of the painting by Juan de Roelas in the Fine Art Museum in Seville.

Also on display in the chapel are six of the twelve candlesticks donated along with other treasures by Juan Antonio Vizarrón y Eguiarreta, Archbishop of Mexico and Viceroy of New Spain. The candlesticks, popularly known as 'los Bizarrones', in honour of their donor, were made in Mexico by Andrés Segura in 1741, and were delivered to the cathedral in 1753.

Sacristía Mayor

The Sacristía Mayor (Main Sacristy) forms part of an extensive building project that included the Sacristía de los Cálices, the Patio de los Óleos, a chapterhouse and another courtyard. All were designed by Diego de Riaño in 1528 and started two years later. After the architect's death in 1534, Martín de Gainza took over and the project was completed in 1543.

Against the walls of the vestibule leading to the Sacristía Mayor are two large wooden cupboards with reliefs of biblical themes and images of female saints carved by Pedro Duque Cornejo in 1743. In them is stored the silver altar used in ceremonies held at Corpus Christi. On the left-hand wall of the vestibule hangs *St Anthony with the Christ Child*, attributed to Francisco de Zurbarán.

The doorway leading to the sacristy is framed by large balusters standing on pedestals and topped with triangular capitals. The decorative scheme incorporates exuberant animal and plant motifs, and images representing Hope and Charity. The wooden doors (1547-49), designed by the sculptor Diego Guillén Ferrant and carved by several different craftsmen, are decorated with medallions showing the Four Evangelists; niches are decorated with carvings of Seville's patron saints St Isidore and St Leander, St Justa and St Rufina. The lower parts of the doors are carved with yet more plant motifs.

The underside of the oblique arch leading into the sacristy is inlaid with caissons, each of which contains relief mouldings of dishes of meat, fish, fruit, vegetables, sweetmeats, jars, goblets or a bag of coins. The sacristy itself takes the shape of a Greek cross with rather short arms and rounded angles. At the southern

Above: Façade of the Sacristía Mayor from the Plaza del Triunfo

Overleaf: Diego de Riaño and Martín de Gainza, vaults above the Sacristía Mayor (1529-43)

end (that facing the door), the sacristy extends beyond the altar area through an arcade; steps lead up to a rectangular space divided into five sections. The elevation consists of pilasters raised on a tall plinth. The shafts vary in design; some are braided, others fluted or decorated with plant and animal motifs. Together they support an entablature with an ornamental frieze. Above are four oval windows, with a blind window in the north wall. A dome crowned by a lantern rises above the central space, and fan vaults extend above the arms of the cross. The altar area is divided by columns, with a semi-dome above the central section and coffered vaulting over the other sections.

The whole sacristy is decorated with splendid ornamental reliefs, which symbolize a single theme – the history of humanity and religious belief, from the Creation to the Last Judgement. They range from simple geometric shapes, such as squares, circles and crosses, through to figures representing the Virtues, the Fathers of the Church and local patron saints protruding from the frieze, to apostles and bishops, and Old Testament priests and prophets distributed around the dome and in the fan vaults. The Last Judgement appears in the dome, and the figure of God the Father in the lantern.

The reliefs in the vaulting above the altar depart from the overall theme, the most predominant being representations of the Assumption and the Twelve Apostles. This theme is picked up again in the motifs on the friezes and the medallions on the side walls. The reliefs are what are known as 'types and antitypes', which portray Old

Testament incidents (types) and corresponding events from the New Testament (antitypes), the Law of Moses contrasting with Christian ethics, the Garden of Eden with the New Jerusalem, and Genesis with the Apocalypse.

The cathedral's most precious works of art have for centuries been kept in the Sacristía Mayor and the Sacristía de los Cálices. At the south side of the Sacristía Mayor are three predellas from altars dismantled in the nineteenth century, which now provide the bases for showcases containing various reliquaries and small carved figures. Above them are three very interesting paintings. In the centre is a magnificent panel by Pedro de Campaña, signed and dated 1547, which depicts the Descent from the Cross; it was inspired by an engraving by Marcantonio Raimondi but far outstrips the latter in its dramatic intensity. It was painted for the now-defunct Church of Santa Cruz, from where it was brought to the cathedral in 1814. To the left hangs *The Martyrdom of St Lawrence*, attributed to Lucas Jordán, and to the right, *St Teresa* by Francisco de Zurbarán.

The paintings on the side walls are also very fine. To the left of the entrance is an early seventeenth-century painting of St Justa and St Rufina by Miguel Esquivel. The work is of special interest because it is the first known treatment of a subject that Murillo would later use in his work for Seville's Capuchin Monastery. The Giralda, standing between the two saints, is a reference to the legend telling how they miraculously intervened to protect the tower during the earthquake of 1504. The clay pots at their feet allude to the fact that the two women sold ceramics for a

Opposite, left: Pedro de
Campaña, *Christ descending
from the Cross* (1547),
Sacristía Mayor

Opposite, right: Miguel Esquivel,
St Justa and St Rufina (ca. 1620),
Sacristía Mayor

Below: Bartolomé Esteban
Murillo, *St Isidore* (1655),
Sacristía Mayor

living, which would later lead to their imprisonment and martyrdom. Next to this painting is *Christ Appearing to St Ignatius Loyola*, thought to date from around 1600 and reminiscent of the works of Alonso Vázquez. *St Isidore* (1655), one of the magnificent paintings by Murillo owned by the cathedral, hangs in the centre of the left-hand wall. The painting wonderfully portrays the saint deep in concentration as he reads. His face is thought to be that of the scholar Juan López de Tabalán. Next to it is *The Immaculate Conception*, dated 1621 and attributed to Pedro de Raxis, a native of Granada. On the right-hand wall is *Our Lady of Mercy*, painted by Juan de Roelas around 1624. Murillo's *St Leander*, also painted in 1655, hangs opposite his *St Isidore*. According to tradition his face is a portrait of the scholar Alonso de Herrera. In his hands St Leander holds a document referring to the campaign against the Arian Heresy. The next painting is Juan Sánchez Cotán's 1620 *Vision of St Francis*. On the north wall is Francisco Bayeu's *Pietà*, signed and dated 1788.

The two sculptures in the sacristy are of St Ferdinand, by Pedro Roldán, commissioned to celebrate the canonization of Ferdinand III in 1671, and of the Immaculate Conception by Alonso Martínez, dating from around 1657.

Various silver statues stand on the chests of drawers on either side of the sacristy. On the right is a bust of St Rosalia, patron saint of Palermo, Sicily, by Antonino Lorenzo Castelli, a silversmith based in that city. On the left are reliquaries in the

form of busts of two of Seville's patron saints, Pius and Laureano, attributed to Juan Laureano de Pina and dating from the late seventeenth century.

Two particularly notable pieces of silverware on display in the sacristy are a pair of huge candlesticks, known as Los Gigantes (The Giants), made by Hernando de Ballesteros the Younger between 1579 and 1581. However, the most important and striking piece of silverware in the sacristy is the great processional monstrance. The religious imagery carved on the monstrance was devised by Canon Francisco Pacheco and executed by Juan de Arfe, whose signature appears on the base and reads '*Joan de Arphe y Villafañe, natural de León, hizo esta obra. Año 1587*' ('Juan de Arfe y Villafañe, native of León, made this piece in the year 1587'). The monstrance consists of a circular base above which rise three circular elements of decreasing size. The piece is decorated with scenes from the Old Testament, figures of the Fathers of the Church, numerous saints and the Lamb of the Apocalypse. Together they symbolize the doctrines of the Council of Trent, proclaiming the triumph of the Eucharist over the Protestant heresy. An allegorical group representing Faith was

Above: Pedro Roldán, *St Ferdinand* (1671), Sacristía Mayor

Left: Antonino Lorenzo Castelli, Reliquary bust of St Rosalia (ca. 1685), Sacristía Mayor

Right: Juan de Arfe,
Processional monstrance
(1580-7), Sacristía Mayor

Below: Antonio Méndez, Lignum
Crucis of Pope Clement XIV
(1796), Sacristía Mayor

replaced in 1668 by an image of the Immaculate Conception by the silversmith Juan
de Segura, who also added a second base with vases of lilies, the figures of angels in
the first and fourth sections, and the statue of Faith Triumphant on the crest.

Four large showcases hold many other important objects. In the first on the left
are pectoral crosses and archiepiscopal rings, and a Lignum Crucis reliquary
(reliquary of the True Cross), which incorporates the pectoral cross of Pope
Clement XIV. The reliquary was made in 1796 by Antonio Méndez and shows two
cherubs supporting the Cross, and two larger angels holding up a globe engraved
with a *mapa mundi* (map of the world). This showcase also contains caskets
holding the relics of the martyrs St Servando and St Germain and the confessor
St Florencio, made by Hernando Ballesteros the Elder and dated 1558.

The second showcase holds a unique piece, the Tablas Anfonsíes, a thirteenth-
century reliquary in the form of a triptych made of wooden panels overlaid with
silver-gilt; this was traditionally attributed to the silversmith Juan de Toledo and
donated to the cathedral by Alfonso X in 1284. The front compartments contain
relics behind rock crystal and enamel. On the reverse side are the heraldic

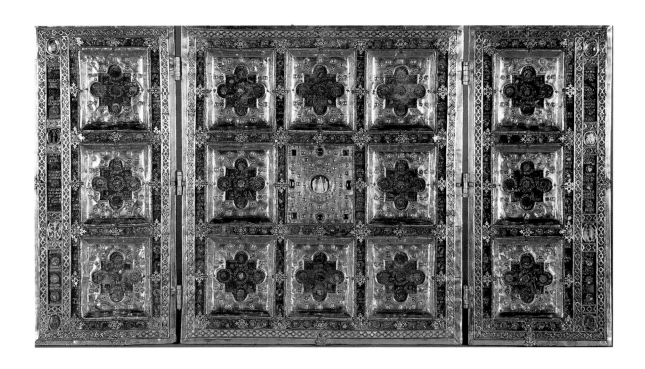

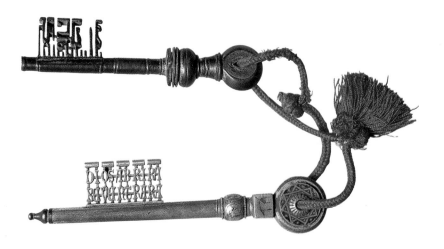

Above: Tablas Alfonsíes
(thirteenth century),
Sacristía Mayor

Left: Keys of Seville
(thirteenth century),
Sacristía Mayor

Right: Banner with images of the Giralda (late seventeenth-century)

Below: sixteenth-century carpet

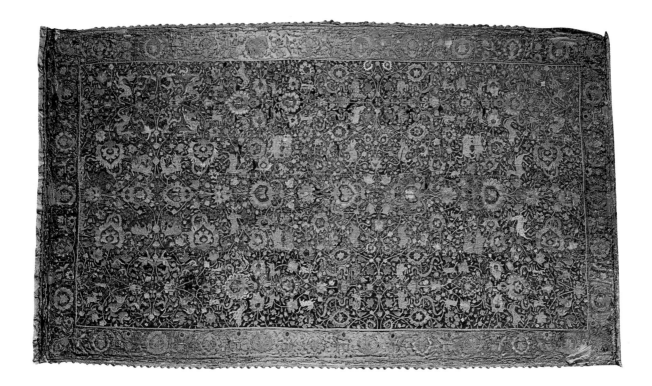

medallions bearing the insignia of Castile and León, and reliefs depicting the Annunciation and the Adoration of the Magi. Displayed next to the reliquary are the keys of the city of Seville; one of silver and bearing an inscription in Hebrew and Latin, and the other of iron and inscribed with Arabic characters. According to tradition, they were handed over to Ferdinand III by King Axataf at the surrender of Seville in 1248.

The third showcase contains a selection from the cathedral treasury's collection of more than 3,000 liturgical artefacts and vestments. They include 300 copes, more than 200 chasubles, 100 dalmatics and many albs and altar cloths. Also in the textile collection is a late sixteenth-century set, which is woven in sturdy drill and comprises a carpet and two hassocks; the altar cloth of Leo X, dating from the early part of the same century; a funeral pall embroidered with the coat-of-arms of the cathedral chapter, made by Francisco Rivera in 1679; the curtains of the eighteenth-century float on which the Grand Monstrance was carried in procession at Corpus Christi; and a Corpus Christi banner from the same period. The most ancient piece in the cathedral's collection of textiles is the Pennant of St Ferdinand, dating from around 1240, though many times restored. The fourth showcase contains a collection of reliquaries in the shape of miniature temples made by Francisco de Alfaro in the 1600s, and another Lignum Crucis reliquary, in the shape of a cross with the scene of the Emtombment, donated by Cardinal Pedro Gómez de Albornoz in 1389.

Patio de los Óleos

The small rectangular space between the Sacristía Mayor and the Sacristía de los
Cálices is known as the Patio de los Óleos (Patio of Oils), after the sacramental oils
that are stored here. It was begun by Diego de Riaño in 1529, and was completed
eight years later by Martín de Gainza. A double arcade extends around three
sides, while the fourth side abuts part of the south-eastern side of the cathedral.
The arcade rests on columns without capitals and is supported by brackets.
While the upper part of the ceiling is plain, the lower part is coffered. The staircase
to the upper level is on the north side of the patio, above the small chapels at the
southern end of the Sacristía de los Cálices.

Capilla del Mariscal

The Capilla del Mariscal (Chapel of the Marshal) takes its name from Diego
Caballero, marshal of the island of Hispaniola, who commissioned the altarpiece in
1555. It was made by the sculptor Pedro de Becerril, to a design thought to be by
Martín de Gainza. It consists of a predella, central section and cresting, and is
framed by pilasters, the outermost of which each support two small statues, of St
Peter and St Paul. The altarpiece celebrates the Purification of the Virgin, depicted
in the central section. On the right are St James and St Dominic, and on the left St
Ildefonso of Toledo and St Francis. Pedro de Campaña, the artist responsible for
the paintings in the altarpiece, seems to have followed suggestions made by
Caballero himself and used the Raphaelesque style that was fashionable in Seville at
the time. However, for the portraits in the predella, he chose a more realistic style;
the subject matter here is Jesus with the Doctors of the Church, with portraits of
the benefactor and members of his family on either side. The Crucifixion and
Resurrection appear on the cresting. The painting of the decorative elements in the
altarpiece is attributed to Antonio de Arfián.

The railing of the tribune on which the altarpiece stands was built in 1571 by
Bartolomé Morel. The chapel's stained-glass window, designed by Arnao de Flandes
and dating from 1556, depicts the Betrothal of Mary and Joseph. The *reja* at the
entrance to the chapel was made in 1555 by Pedro Delgado to a design by Martín
de Gainza.

Above: Pedro Delgado, *Christ
placed in the Tomb*, cresting of the
reja (1555), Capilla del Mariscal

Opposite: Pedro de Campaña,
The Purification of the Virgin (1555-6),
Capilla del Mariscal

Hernán Ruiz the Younger and
Asensio de Maeda, Antechamber
of the Chapterhouse (1558-85)

Antecabildo

Through a doorway designed by Asensio de Maeda, and across a small rectangular vestibule – with a flat ceiling decorated with reliefs of Christ and the Madonna, David and Solomon – the Capilla del Mariscal leads to the Antecabildo, the antechamber of the chapterhouse. The Antecabildo in turn provides access to the chapterhouse and the chapterhouse courtyard.

The Antecalbildo was designed by Hernán Ruiz the Younger. Work began in 1558 and continued until 1585, when the ceiling, designed by Juan de Minjares and Asensio de Maeda, was completed. The north and south walls have a symmetrical arrangement: the lower section with doors and windows and the upper area with reliefs, inscriptions and skylights. The long east and west walls contain a series of doors, both real and false, and inscribed tablets. Above them are reliefs and niches with statues, each flanked by pairs of Ionic pilasters. The room has a vaulted, coffered ceiling with a central lantern and a second, modern skylight at the southern end. Black slate emphasizes the division of the walls and outlines the geometric framework of the ceiling.

The statues in the niches are of classical female figures representing the Virtues: Providence, Charity, Justice, Hope, Temperance, Fortitude and Prudence. Two of these are documented as works of Diego de Pesquera, and one is probably by the same artist. The rest are attributed to Juan Bautista Vázquez the Elder. Pesquera also executed the reliefs of the Four Evangelists above the entrance and the exit to the courtyard. The medallions on the north and south walls, which show scenes from the life of Noah, may be the work of followers of Vázquez the Elder. The identity of the sculptor of the reliefs on the east and west walls is uncertainly known but their style suggests that they may be attributable to Pesquera, Vázquez the Elder and Diego de Velasco. While some of the subjects that they depict are somewhat unclear, others are obviously scenes from the Old and New Testaments: they include the Israelites crossing the Red Sea, Haman condemned to death, Aaron and Moses performing miracles before Pharaoh, the Whore of Babylon, the Tower of Babel, Pentecost, Wisdom before the Sciences and the Arts, Jesus teaching in the Temple, the Seven Deadly Sins, and Virtue conquering the Vices. The reliefs, together with the Latin inscriptions devised by Canon Francisco Pacheco, constitute a series of humanistic instructions that were intended as a code of conduct for members of the cathedral chapter. It reminds them that, in the administration of cathedral affairs, they should always act with justice and not allow themselves to be seduced by worldly considerations.

Patio del Cabildo

The imaginatively designed Patio del Cabildo (Chapterhouse Courtyard) leads to the Sacristía Mayor and the Sala de Columnas (Colonnaded Hall), so called because of the series of columns running along its length. The Patio del Cabildo is a square space whose east and west walls are symmetrically pierced with a series of doorways, both real and false. The northern and southern walls are punctuated by asymmetrically arranged alcoves, which appear to have been moved to the west in order to incorporate the doors leading into the chapterhouse. The doorways on the east and west walls are in two distinctive styles. All incorporate black slate and several are decorated with medallions and figures of children and cherubim. The flat ceiling is decorated with a variety of geometric patterns. Like the adjoining Cabildo and Antecabildo, the Patio del Cabildo was designed by Hernán Ruiz the Younger, and building work on the courtyard ran parallel with their construction. Within the Patio del Cabildo is the Custodia Chica, a small silver monstrance designed by Francisco de Alfaro in the early seventeenth century and said to contain relics of the True Cross and the Crown of Thorns. It is set on a Baroque silver pedestal dating from the second half of the eighteenth century. The four silver vases with bunches of flowers date from the same period. Also on display here is the wooden model that was Juan de Arfe's winning entry for the competition organized by the cathedral chapter in 1580 to find a craftsman to build the Great Monstrance.

Hernán Ruiz II, Patio del Cabildo

Sala Capitular

From the Antecabildo, a narrow corridor leads to the Sala Capitular (Chapterhouse). At the chapterhouse door, the darkness of the corridor, with its double row of pilasters and flat coffered ceiling, is suddenly dispelled by light streaming in from a lantern and a single window; this gives a surprising sensation of space.

The double colonnade of Doric and Ionic pilasters in the corridor is repeated in the Sala Capitular, whose elliptical ground plan was already ahead of Italian experimentation with this shape. On the lower level, however, the need to provide a bench to seat members of the chapter made it necessary for the columns to be somewhat shorter. The fluted Ionic pillars stand on pedestals and the lower sections are decorated with plant and animal motifs. Between the columns are a series of paintings and Latin inscriptions, while large reliefs set within arches alternate with rectangular panels framed by inscriptions. Rising above the cornice is an oval coffered ceiling pierced by a lantern. The lower row of caissons contain *oeil-de-boeuf* (bull's eye) windows and a series of paintings. This is a ceiling of great structural complexity and a supreme example of the skill of Renaissance stonemasons.

The Sala Capitular was designed by Hermán Ruiz the Younger. Construction began in 1558, continuing until 1592, when Asensio de Maeda laid the trompe l'oeil marble floor, based on Michelangelo's design for the Piazza del Campidoglio in Rome. Juan Bautista Vázquez the Elder, Diego de Velasco and Marcos Cabrera were responsible for the sculptures. Vázquez and Velasco created the large reliefs of the Assumption, the Vision of the Mystic Lamb, St John with the Angel with Feet as Pillars of Fire, Christ Casting out the Moneylenders, the Vision of the Angels with Trumpets, the Vision of the Seven Candlesticks, the Smoke Rising from the Bottomless Pit and the Heavenly Father with the Harvesters. The rectangular reliefs, all by Marcos Cabrera, show Christ calming the storm on the Sea of Tiberius, the Agony in the Garden, St Peter with the Unclean Animals, Christ Preaching to His Disciples, Daniel in the Lions' Den, the Baptism of Christ and the Parable of the Sower. The Latin inscriptions above and below the reliefs refer to the scenes they depict. The murals between the Ionic pilasters, representing the Virtues, were painted by Pablo Céspedes in 1592. With those in the Antecabildo, this corpus of sculpted and painted images, and the Latin inscriptions were intended to form a complex and erudite reminder to members of the chapter of their obligations and the moral code that they were required to observe. This set of rules, designed to ensure wise administration of cathedral affairs, was also devised by Canon Francisco Pacheco.

In 1667, as a finishing touch to repairs carried out in the Sala Capitular, Murillo was commissioned to restore the paintings by Céspedes and was asked to provide new circular reliefs for the dome; Murillo's eight circular reliefs show Seville's saints, Justa, Pius, Isidore, Hermenegild, Ferdinand, Leander, Laureano and Rufina, some of them modelled on his earlier works. He was also asked to paint an Immaculate Conception. The result is one of the artist's finest interpretations of this theme. The sumptuous frame of gilded and polychromed wood was made by Bernardo Simón de Pineda. The painting was placed on the wall of the Sala Capitular in 1668, positioned so as to provide a focal point in what had previously been a somewhat undefined expanse, so transforming the whole spatial concept of the chapterhouse. To create this effect, one of the windows had to be closed off.

Page 110: Hernán Ruiz the Younger and Asensio de Maeda, Chapterhouse (1558-92)

Page 111: Floor of the Chapterhouse (1591)

The only pieces of furniture in the Sala Capitular are the archbishop's mahogany throne, which until recently was adorned with small figures of Faith, Hope and Charity carved by Diego de Velasco in 1592; and a secretary's bench, also by Velasco, with reliefs of angels in a style reminiscent of Michelangelo decorating both sides of the backrest.

Casa de Cuentas

The Casa de Cuentas (Counting House) is entered from the Capilla del Mariscal, through a doorway designed by Hernán Ruiz the Younger. The ground-floor room has a wooden coffered ceiling and doors in either wall, one leading to the outside, the other giving access to the corridor of the Sala Capitular and the stairway to the upper floor.

The room now houses precious items from the cathedral treasury. Built up from acquisitions and commissions by the cathedral chapter, and numerous private donations, it contains pieces ranging in style from Gothic to present-day; it is one of the richest in Spain.

Among the silverware in the showcases, the most outstanding is that displayed above the entrance: a statue of St Joseph by Pedro Roldán, flower vases attributed to Juan de Arellano, and the *Vocation of St Matthew* and *St John the Baptist before the Sanhedrin*, both by Luis Valdés. Notable among the Gothic pieces is the reliquary of Philip V of France and Jeanne of Burgundy, which is modelled in the shape of the church, whose exquisitely enamelled doors open to reveal a gilt statue of the Madonna and Child. The reliquary dates from between 1317 and 1322, and may have been made in the workshops of the Paris school. Another Gothic piece is the fourteenth-century rock crystal goblet decorated with silver gilt.

The imposing altar cross has maker's marks on the shaft, which indicate that it was made between 1486 and 1502. The cross and the Alfonsí candlesticks form part of an altar set donated by Cardinal Hurtado de Mendoza. The upper section of the cross is a later replacement, although the original crucifix remains.

The pax showing St Anne and the Madonna and Child dates from the first quarter of the sixteenth century and is attributed to Martín de Oñate, who was active in Seville between 1506 and 1523. It came from the Church of St Anne and bears one of the oldest Sevillian maker's marks. The Giralda, as it appears here, does not feature the belfry added by Hernán Ruiz the Younger. The so-called Constantine Reliquary containing the Lignum Crucis was a gift from Archbishop Alonso de Fonseca and dates from the same period.

The pax with the Assumption of the Virgin and with the Ascension of Christ were both made in 1556 by Hernando de Ballesteros. Like many others made during the Renaissance, they are shaped like miniature altarpieces. Other Renaissance pieces include the holy oil containers, with hallmarks of workshops in the city of Antwerp, and the water jug with a spout in the form of a serpent, a handle in the form of a lizard and a dragon on the lid. Both the oil containers and the jug were acquired by the cathedral chapter in 1564.

The San Millán de la Cogolla reliquary was made in Mexico and is dated 1578. It was commissioned by Doña María de la Torre and donated to the cathedral by Canon Francisco Mateos Gago. The so-called Merino patriarchal cross, used as the

Left: Ignacio Thamaral, monstrance of Doña de Isabel Pérez Caro (1729)

Below: Damián de Castro., chalice of Archbishop Delgado y Venegas (1777)

Right: St John Nepomuk
Monstrance signed 'X.J' (1780)

Below: Luis Valadier and
Francisco Leclare, Maundy
Thursday urn (1774)

cathedral's processional cross, has formed part of the cathedral treasury since the late sixteenth century. The cathedral chapter purchased it from Merino, a silversmith in Jaén, in 1587.

The treasury contains many major eighteenth-century works. The gold monstrance by Ignacio Tharamal, decorated with diamonds, pearls and rubies, with exquisite angel heads at the base, is a fine example of Spanish craftsmanship of the first half of the century. It was donated by Doña Isabel Pérez Caro and was used for the first time in the Corpus Christi procession of 1729. The chalice and set of salvers donated by Archbishop Delgado y Venegas are particularly fine. The golden chalice, made by Damián de Castro, and first used on Maundy Thursday 1777, amply demonstrates Castro as the foremost exponent of the Rococo style in silverware. The set of salvers, also by Castro and with the coat-of-arms of Archbishop Delgado y Venegas in the centre, are equally important pieces; the moulded rim and the swathes of ribbon on the inner surface lend the salvers typical Rococo vitality. The urn from the Maundy Thursday monument was commissioned by Canon Juan Ignacio del Rosal and made in Rome by Luis Valadier; the pedestal was made by Francisco Leclare in 1774. The monstrance of Cardinal Solis came to the treasury in 1780. It is known both as the Great Monstrance and the St John Nepomuk Monstrance, because of the image of the saint on the shaft and the scenes from his life on the base. An inscription reveals that it was made in Rome in 1775. The golden censer made by the silversmith Antonio Méndez was first seen in public at the Corpus Christi procession of 1791. It was donated to the cathedral by the merchant Manuel Paulín de la Barrera.

Artefacts of the nineteenth century, already well represented by the church furnishings displayed in the various showcases within the cathedral, are represented in the treasury's collection by two magnificent silver statues, one of St Ferdinand, the other of St Louis of France, and the large chalice in Empire Style. Among pieces dating from the twentieth century is the silver crown made by Pedro Vives y Ferrer for the Virgen de los Reyes and commissioned by Archbishop Marcelo.

Eastern Chapels

Above the keystones of the arches leading to the chapels in the east end are two large medallions. According to tradition, these represent the knights Garcí and Diego Pérez de Vargas, comrades-in-arms of Fernando III, who played a leading role in the conquest of Seville. Appearing in the two rows of niches in the presbytery are figures of the Four Evangelists, and the local saints Isidore, Leander, Justa and Rufina. Figures of St Peter and St Paul stand on either side of the altar, above which is a relief showing the Vision of Isaiah.

Capilla de las Santas Justa y Rufina

The Capilla de las Santas Justa y Rufina, dedicated to two of Seville's patron saints Justa and Rufina, seems to have been founded in 1622 when the Bécquer brothers donated the *reja* inscribed with the words *'Esta capilla y entierro es de Miguel y Adán Bécquer hermanos y de sus herederos y sucesores. Año 1622'* ('This chapel and tomb belongs to the brothers Miguel and Adán Bécquer, their heirs and successors. 1622').

The statues of the two stands, carved by Pedro Duque Cornejo in 1728 and now kept on the altar, were originally in the parish church of El Divino Salvador in Seville. Interestingly, the Giralda that stands between them, made by Juan de Dios, is shown as it appeared at the beginning of the eighteenth century. Since they were moved to the cathedral in the nineteenth century, the statues have been carried in processions at Corpus Christi. The painting of St Roche above the entrance is attributed to Antonio de Arfián.

Capilla de Santa Bárbara

This tiny chapel, endowed in 1544 by Canon Rodrigo de Solís of Seville, is dominated by the altarpiece built in 1554 by Antón Ruiz, a minor follower of Pedro de Villegas. The central panel shows the Holy Family, with the Twelve Apostles and the Pentecost represented on the sides. An eighteenth-century sculpture of St Anthony of Padua stands to one side.

Capilla de la Concepción Grande

As the stone tablet on the left wall confirms, the Capilla de la Concepción Grande (Great Chapel of the Immaculate Conception) was founded in the mid-seventeenth century by the Sepúlveda family.

The altarpiece was designed by the sculptor Francisco Dionisio de Rivas, and completed in 1658 by Martín Moreno. The barley-sugar columns, decorated with vine tendrils and bunches of grapes, provide a framework for the large crucifix in the

Above: Pedro Duque Cornejo,
St Justa and St Rufina (1728),
Capilla de Santas Justa y Rufina

Opposite: Alonso Martínez,
The Immaculate Conception,
Capilla de la Concepción Grande

upper section, an anonymous work dating from the late fifteenth or early sixteenth century. The statues of St Joseph, St Paul, St Gonzalo and St Anthony of Padua were made by Alonso Martínez, who also carved the central figure of the Immaculate Conception.

Since the 1880s, the chapel has housed the tomb of Cardinal Francisco Javier Cienfuegos y Jovellanos, designed by the architect Manuel Portillo. The recumbent figure of the cardinal lies on a large marble sarcophagus, decorated with figures symbolizing the Theological Virtues.

The chapel is fronted by a *reja* painted, and possibly also made, by Juan de Valdés Leal. To him is also ascribed the large marble tablet on the left-hand wall, decorated with bronze and alluding to the foundation of the chapel. On the right-hand wall is *The Slaughter of the Innocents* by Jacopo Fardella.

Opposite: Martín de Gainza, Capilla Real (1551-3)

Page 122: The Virgin of the Kings (13th century), Capilla Real

Page 123: Juan Laureano de Pina, The urn of St Ferdinand (1690), Capilla Real

Capilla Real

The Capilla Real (Royal Chapel) occupies the eastern end of the cathedral; it is based on a square ground plan with a semicircular wall, and with a chapel and a sacristy on either side. The entrance to the Capilla Real is through a large semicircular arch above which are a series of niches containing figures of the Kings of Judah. The great *reja* was commissioned by Charles III and designed in 1766 by Sebastian van de Borcht, as the inscription on the upper frieze records; the date that it bears (1773) almost certainly refers to the year the work was completed. The *reja* is crowned by a sculpture by Jerónimo Roldán, which shows Ferdinand III receiving the keys of Seville from King Axataf.

Close to the entrance, on either side of the chapel, are the tombs of Alfonso X the Wise, and his mother Beatrice of Swabia. The niches, which date from the same period as the tombs, are adorned with military trophies, figures representing the Virtues and the coats-of-arms of Castile and León, and are topped with the figure of Fame. The praying figures of the king and his mother were not added until 1948; that of Alfonso X is by Antonio Cano and Carmen Jiménez, and that of Beatrice of Swabia is by Juan Luis Vasallo. Before the statues were installed, the simple wooden coffins containing the royal remains were covered with brocaded cloth, with the crowns and sceptres of the deceased resting on cushions.

The coffered dome covering the central space of the Capilla Real is decorated with busts of kings and discs resting on scallops. A large scallop with figures of angels stands above the presbytery; above the side chapels are virtually flat vaults adorned with plant motifs. Angels with musical instruments and children carrying halberds occupy the frieze. The internal walls are divided by eight huge pilasters, with figures representing the Virtues and Apostles carved on their lower sections.

The construction of the chapel was very long and drawn out. In 1489 the master builder Alonso Rodríguez was involved in discussions about the type of materials to be used in the building. In 1515, Enrique Egas and Juan de Álava were asked to submit plans. Further plans were drawn up by Juan Gil and Martín de Gainza and, although Alonso de Covarrubias started work on some of them, building itself did not begin until 1551; the project had been put out to tender and had been awarded to Martín de Gainza, who had been obliged to produce new drawings and who directed construction until his death in 1556. In the same year, during the erection of

the perimeter walls and the vault above the presbytery, problems emerged with the cementation. Hernán Ruiz the Younger, appointed cathedral architect in 1557, ordered work to be suspended until 1562. He then went on to supervise the construction of the great coffered dome above the chapel's central space and the doorways to the sacristies. Unable to finish the work, he was succeeded by Pedro Díaz de Palacios and Juan and Asensio de Maeda. Although the basic structure was finished in 1575, it was another four years before the royal remains were transferred to the chapel and some of the building work continued into the next decade. From 1754 onwards, more features were added, including Sebastian van der Borcht's reconstruction of the lantern on top of the dome.

A large number of artists were responsible for the sculptures in the chapel, the most outstanding being Pedro de Campos and Lorenzo de Bao, who carved the figures of the Kings of Judah on the arch at the entrance, and the relief of the Vision of Isaiah. These were based on sketches by the painter Pedro de Campaña. The figures of St Justa and St Rufina are by Diego de Pesquera, and those of the Evangelists are attributed to Juan Marín.

The stained-glass windows at the sides of the chapel, showing royal coats-of-arms, are by the Flemish craftsman Vicente Menardo, who began work in 1574. The windows have been restored on several occasions.

The altarpiece dominating the Capilla Real was built by the woodcarver Luis Ortiz de Vargas between 1643 and 1649. The Virgen de los Reyes (Virgin of the Kings) with the Infant Jesus on her lap occupies the central niche. The two figures, beneath a silver canopy, date from the thirteenth century and show distinct French Gothic influences. They are fitted with an internal wooden mechanism to make their heads and hands move. The side panels of the altarpiece are occupied by seventeenth-century carvings of St Joachim and St Anne.

The altar frontal is an important piece of Baroque silverwork. The central section was made by Juan Laureano de Pina in 1719 and reconstructed in 1739 by José de Villaviciosa. The embossed side panels are by the silversmith Domínguez and also date from 1719. The double eagle candelabra on the side tables are the work of eighteenth-century Peruvian silversmiths.

The silver gilt and crystal urn, which stands on the altar of the Virgen de los Reyes and contains the remains of St Ferdinand, is regarded as the greatest masterpiece produced by the goldsmiths of Seville during the Baroque era. It was started in 1690 by Juan Laureano de Pina, and several other goldsmiths worked on it before its completion in 1719. The urn is usually kept closed but can be opened to show the relics of the canonized king. The altar frontal on which it stands is a fine example of the work of the silversmiths Resiente and Villaviciosa.

On either side of the urn are staircases leading to the crypt, which is used as the royal vault and which contains the remains of various members of the Spanish royal family, including Pedro I of Castile and his wife María de Padilla. On a small altar is the ivory statue of the Virgen de las Batallas (Virgin of the Battles). This thirteenth-century figure of the Madonna and Child shows clear French influences. According to tradition, she was carried into battle by Ferdinand III during his various military campaigns against the Moors.

In the chapel on the left is an altarpiece built by Juan de Torres in 1648, dominated by an *Ecce Homo* signed by Francisco Terrili. Opposite is a large glass case

Francisco de Zurbarán,
The Immaculate Conception
(ca. 1630), Capilla de San Pedro

containing some major pieces of silverware, including some fine chalices and salvers from various periods ranging from the sixteenth to the twentieth centuries.

From this chapel a small door leads into the sacristy, where a number of objects relating to Ferdinand III are preserved, one being the king's sword. Among the paintings on display here are a copy of Murillo's *St Ferdinand* and of his *Our Lady of Sorrows*. Two late seventeenth-century works are also shown: one a painting of the Virgen de los Reyes and the other a canvas showing St Joseph with a garland of flowers. The Neo-classical organ on the chapel tribune was built in 1807 by Antonio Otin Calvete.

The chapel on the right houses Luis de Figueroa's altarpiece of 1638, with a statue of St Anthony. The late eighteenth-century choir stalls and lectern were donated by Charles IV, who also gave the gilt bronze candlestick and cross in the presbytery.

Capilla de San Pedro

The Capilla de San Pedro (Chapel of St Peter) dates from the sixteenth century. The altarpiece was commissioned by the Marquess of Malagón, designed by Miguel de Zumárraga and carved by the Diego López Bueno between 1620 and 1625; the gilding is by the painters Baltasar Quintero and Vicente Perea. The paintings lining the altarpiece, by Francisco de Zurbarán, show scenes from the life of St Peter and the Immaculate Conception. They are thought to have been executed some time after 1625 and are among the first works that the artist executed in Seville. They are particularly impressive on account of the sombre dignity and realism of the figures. The Immaculate Conception is one of Zurbarán's greatest achievements.

More fine paintings appear on the right-hand wall. The most outstanding among them is a series of scenes from the life of St Peter Nolasco. Although the work has always been attributed to Francisco Reina, the recent discovery of traces of a signature, part of which suggests the name of Juan Luis Zambrano, has led some authorities to believe that he was the artist responsible. On the same wall are two canvases from the Bolognese school, *The Martyrdom of St Agnes* and *The Liberation of St Peter*, by followers of Alessandro Tiarini. Also noteworthy is the *Repentance of St Peter*, a painting of the Flemish school reminiscent of the works of Gerard Seghers.

The tomb in the chapel is that of Archbishop Diego de Deza, brought here in 1884 when Seville's Santo Tomás school, of which he was the founder, was demolished. The effigy of the recumbent archbishop is all that remains of the original tomb, dating from around 1523, the year of his death. The rest was constructed around 1884.

The *reja* fronting the chapel was designed in 1778 by the Franciscan friar José Cordero. It is based on the *reja* of the Capilla de la Concepción Grande, with the addition of the Papal Crown and Apostolic Keys to the cresting.

Altar de la Asunción

Both the altarpiece and the *reja* of the Altar de la Asunción (Altar of the Assumption) date from around 1593. In the centre of the altarpiece is a high relief of the Assumption of the Virgin. The remaining paintings of angels inside the arch, and the Prophets and Fathers of the Church on the predella, are by Alonso

Vázquez. To the sides of the altar are portraits of members of the family of the chapel's donor, Don Juan Cristóbal de la Puebla. The tiled altar frontal dates from the late sixteenth century.

Altar de la Magdalena

The Altar de la Magdalena (Altar of Mary Magdalene) was founded in 1537 by Don Pedro García de Villadiego and his wife Catalina Rodríguez. The paintings on the altarpiece are by a follower of Alejo Fernández. The one in the centre shows Christ appearing to Mary Magdalene, while the one in the pediment depicts the Annunciation. Those on the sides show St Catherine and St Barbara, and St Andrew, St James, St Peter and St Paul. On the predella, the donor is seen with St Benedict and his wife with St Francis.

Inside the Puerta de Palos is an interesting stained-glass window made by Arnao de Vergara in 1535. Although it is dedicated to St Sebastian, the face of the saint is, in fact, a portrait of Charles V. Beneath it is a painted panel showing St Sebastian, a mid-sixteenth-century work by Antonio de Arfiá.

Index